"Vaneetha takes on a sensitive, deeply personal, potentially embarrassing reality with clarity and honesty yet without rancor or malice. As someone who has been through a divorce in similar circumstances to hers, I can attest to the painful yet healing accuracy of her wisdom in these pages. And I can attest to the unfailing hope she points the reader to in Christ, without flippancy or pat answers. Prior to this book, I knew of no books on divorce I would actually be willing to hand to a person navigating that devastating reality. Now I have one, and I am grateful for it!"

BARNABAS PIPER, Assistant Pastor, Immanuel Nashville; Author, *Help My Unbelief* and *Hoping for Happiness*

"No one begins a marriage saying, 'I sure hope I'll get to walk through a divorce,' and yet so many of us end up facing the realities of shattered dreams and broken promises. Once again, my friend Vaneetha Risner has parlayed her suffering into deep understanding, scriptural fidelity, and gracious blessing. I strongly recommend this resource, for those who are facing divorce and also for those who are seeking to help."

ELYSE FITZPATRICK, Author, *Friend of Sinners*

"Our God hates divorce. So do his people. We grieve the sin and profound hurt that lead to and come from divorces. As Jesus says, it was not this way from the beginning. Yet mourn them as we do, they happen, and so tragically often in our day, and many of Christ's people are left aching and searching for Christian counsel in their devastation. Vaneetha has not only walked with faith through this devastation but has been courageous enough to answer the call to help other Christians who are hurting. This book is no celebration of divorce but an offer of real, solid Christian hope in the midst of one of life's greatest anguishes. I pray this book will help you move forward in Jesus and draw closer to him in your pain."

DAVID MATHIS, Senior Teacher and Executive Editor, desiringGod.org; Author, *Rich Wounds*

"In a season that is painfully lonely and isolating, Vaneetha's words made me feel seen and even encouraged. With honesty and tenderness, she gave language to the layered ache, confusion, and grief of divorce—especially for a Christian—while offering practical handlebars for traveling through it with faith. This book helped me feel less alone in my pain, and I'll be sharing it with friends who need the reminder that, even in the devastation of divorce, God will never leave us."

BRIGHTON BUTLER, Lifestyle Blogger;
Founder of Brighton the Day

"I wish I had had this book when I was first facing divorce. Vaneetha offers essential wisdom for anyone facing divorce, and her words are helpful for those of us on the other side of it as well. God is kind, and his words are trustworthy. Vaneetha reminds us, in a voice we can hear, of the value of trusting Jesus despite circumstances that seem to knock us off our foundation. I pray this book is shared far and wide."

WENDY ALSUP, Author, *I Forgive You: Finding Peace and Moving Forward When Life Really Hurts*

"As someone who has personally walked through the devastation of divorce, I know the crushing weight of betrayal, the loneliness of an empty home, and the ache of wondering if life will ever feel whole again. For those of us who have endured this pain, resources often fall short—either too abstract and theological to touch the heart or too shallow to offer lasting hope. That is why *This Was Never the Plan* is such a rare and necessary gift. It is tender, timely, and profoundly hopeful. Vaneetha writes not as a detached expert but as a fellow sojourner. This is a trustworthy companion for anyone navigating the heartbreak of divorce."

SHANNON KAY MCCOY, Counselor; Speaker;
Author, *Help! I'm a Slave to Food*

"Biblically rich, wonderfully practical, and searingly honest, this is a book we so badly need. Through the measured use of her own experience, Vaneetha Risner provides a first-hand account of the struggles Christians face when their lives are upended by divorce. Where this book really excels, however, is in its description of the many ways Christ meets us in such struggles. This isn't just a book for those who have experienced divorce; it needs to be read by their friends and by the pastors of their churches."

STEVE MIDGLEY, Executive Director, Biblical Counselling UK; Board Member, CCEF

"If you're holding this book, your heart is wrenching. Vaneetha is a tender guide in this tumultuous time. *This Was Never the Plan* comes alongside you as you grapple with the hard questions and social challenges of processing an unwanted divorce. Allow this book to serve you one page at a time as you walk with God one day at a time."

BRAD HAMBRICK, Pastor of Counseling, The Summit Church, Durham, NC; Author, *True Betrayal: 9 Steps for Processing Your Spouse's Infidelity*

"I am so thankful for this book. Vaneetha offers comfort and hope as she lays open the Scriptures and her own heart. There are no well-worn platitudes or shallow promises but plenty of compassion, wisdom, and grace—and just the right amount of humour. Vaneetha's experience enables her to speak tenderly, and she also offers practical guidance for those navigating the challenges of single parenting, dating, and belonging at church. This will be of enormous help both to those experiencing divorce and those seeking walk to alongside."

CAROLYN LACEY, Women's Worker, Woodgreen Evangelical Church, Worcester, UK; Author, *Say the Right Thing*

"If you are reeling from a divorce you never wanted, *This Was Never the Plan* is a lifeline. In these pages, you will see yourself in Vaneetha's story as she opens her heart and shares the raw, unfiltered emotions of her own unwanted divorce. But Vaneetha doesn't leave you in the pain. With honesty and compassion, she gently guides you along a pathway of healing—helping you move through the heartbreak you feel today toward renewed hope for tomorrow. Her journey is living proof that your heart can heal, your future can be restored, and that divorce doesn't get the last word."

STEVE GRISSOM, Founder of DivorceCare

"This book is deeply moving and profoundly courageous yet genuinely hope-filled. Vaneetha Rendall Risner's journey through the anguish of divorce is painful but vital reading for anyone who has had to trace a similar path, as well as for those walking beside them. You are not alone."

DAVE AND SALLY GOBBETT, Highfields Church, Cardiff, Wales; Authors, *Hallelujah*

"Compassionate, wise, and vulnerably honest, Vaneetha offers women facing divorce both a roadmap for healing and a blueprint for rebuilding. She shows readers not just how to mend a broken heart but how to emerge stronger and healthier—not in spite of their pain but because of it."

LESLIE VERNICK, Relationship Coach; Speaker; Author, *The Emotionally Destructive Relationship* and *The Emotionally Destructive Marriage.*

"With appropriate honesty and God-given grace, Vaneetha Risner shares the heartbreak of divorce and the deeper hope that can be found in Christ. *This Was Never the Plan* offers comfort that will help the wounded and truth that will inform the perplexed. Through it, she guides hurting believers to believe in God's purpose and rest in his love."

TIM CHALLIES, Author, *Seasons of Sorrow*

VANEETHA
RENDALL RISNER

THIS WAS NEVER THE PLAN

WALKING WITH GOD THROUGH THE HEARTACHE OF DIVORCE

This Was Never the Plan

Published by:
The Good Book Company

thegoodbook.com | thegoodbook.co.uk
thegoodbook.com.au | thegoodbook.co.nz

Published in association with the literary agency of Wolgemuth & Wilson.

Cover design by Faceout Studio | Design and art direction by André Parker

ISBN: 9781802544145 | JOB-008574 | Printed in India

For Katie and Kristi,
who lived this story with me
and grew into women I trust and admire.

VANEETHA is passionate about helping others find hope and joy in the midst of suffering. Her story includes contracting polio as a child, losing an infant son unexpectedly, developing post-polio syndrome, going through an unwanted divorce, and struggling as a single parent—all of which have led her to wrestle honestly with loss.

Vaneetha lives in Raleigh, North Carolina and is the author of several books, including *Watching for the Morning* and her memoir, *Walking Through Fire*. She's also a regular contributor to desiringGod.org.

Vaneetha loves to laugh, speaks sarcasm fluently, and is obsessed with colorful office supplies and dark chocolate. You can find more from Vaneetha at her website,

VANEETHA.COM

CONTENTS

FOREWORD

As I read this wonderful book, I felt as if I were standing on holy ground.

It is a rare gift to be invited to eavesdrop on the most private, painful, and self-exposing season in a person's life. To be welcomed to look into the secret pages of a deeply personal journal, to witness a person's struggle with God, and to be there with them as thoughts and emotions come splashing out is a very rare opportunity. We all live such private lives, protectively holding the secrets that live behind private fences and closed doors. We often celebrate alone, grieve alone, and suffer alone, afraid of the judgment and shame that we think would accompany inviting others in. Because we guard our struggles from public exposure, we fail to know the essential help of walking with one another, of learning from one another, and of knowing the miracle of how, in the hands of God, when a weak one walks with a weak one, the result is often renewed strength.

God did not design us to live alone; the earliest history in Genesis makes that very clear. Everyone's life is a community project. Independent health, strength, wisdom, and righteousness are altogether a delusion. So, I

have a deep appreciation for how Vaneetha steps toward us with a transparency that hasn't been redecorated, walking us through the dark hallways of her shattered life. But what is here is not just a chronicle of bitterness, fear, and shame. You won't close this book burdened with grief. You won't leave hopeless, not knowing what to do. Ultimately, this book is about a hope that is deeper and stronger than the worst thing that could ever happen to you.

As I read, I kept thinking of Paul's words in 2 Corinthians 1:3-7:

> *Blessed be the God and Father of our Lord Jesus Christ, the Father of mercies and God of all comfort, who comforts us in all our affliction, so that we may be able to comfort those who are in any affliction, with the comfort with which we ourselves are comforted by God. For as we share abundantly in Christ's sufferings, so through Christ we share abundantly in comfort too. If we are afflicted, it is for your comfort and salvation; and if we are comforted, it is for your comfort, which you experience when you patiently endure the same sufferings that we suffer. Our hope for you is unshaken, for we know that as you share in our sufferings, you will also share in our comfort.*

The apostle Paul says something significant here about our suffering and God's comfort. God meets us with his comfort—a grace we could never have earned—but this comfort has a mission attached to it. God comforts us "so that we may be able to comfort those who are in any affliction." I am so glad that Vaneetha chose not to hide her suffering or hoard the glory of the comfort she received from her ever-present, ever-steadfast, and ever-loving Savior. Paul says to his readers, who will experience the travails of life in this fallen world, "Our hope for you is

unshaken, for we know that as you share in our sufferings, you will also share in our comfort." The comfort that we have received should motivate and mobilize us to be agents of that comfort in the lives of others, and the result of that is unshakable hope. Our plans may end up lying at our feet like shattered glass on a concrete floor, but what God plans to do with those shattered pieces is beautiful and comforting beyond what we could ask or imagine.

But there is another, even more deeply transformative message in this book that you do not want to miss. If I were to summarize the core message of this transparent, helpful, wise, and practical book, here is what it would be: your tragedies, weaknesses, and sins aren't ultimate; God is. He is bigger than any tragedy you will ever face. He is more gloriously beautiful than any ugly thing you will have to endure. He is infinitely more powerful than the most powerful thing you could ever experience. He is never defeated. He is never confused. He is never taken aback or shocked. His plans are never thwarted, his love never runs out, and his forgiving grace is inexhaustible.

As I concluded reading, another passage came to mind:

Though the fig tree should not blossom,
nor fruit be on the vines,
the produce of the olive fail
and the fields yield no food,
the flock be cut off from the fold
and there be no herd in the stalls,
yet I will rejoice in the LORD;
I will take joy in the God of my salvation.
God, the Lord, is my strength;
he makes my feet like the deer's;
he makes me tread on my high places.
(Habakkuk 3:17-19)

These words were written to people living in an agricultural society. If there are no figs, no olive oil, no food in the fields, and no flocks and herds, then life as you have known it is gone. All the normal things you would depend on are no more. But this passage doesn't end with screams of terror; it ends with dances of joy. Why? The answer is clear: because loss isn't ultimate; God is. Because this is true: on the other side of loss, there is strength and joy to be found. So, as you read *This Was Never the Plan*, I hope that you find yourself able to open your heart and be reminded that there is life—real life—on the other side of whatever has died, because your Lord lives. And what he gives, and gives and gives again, is life—real life, which no one and nothing can take from you.

Paul David Tripp
October 2025

CHAPTER 1

THE UNDOING

"Will life ever be good again?"

That was the question I kept asking myself after my separation and divorce. I assumed I'd survive, but would I laugh again? Could I find joy? Or feel a sense of belonging?

The future I'd envisioned was destroyed. I felt lost and alone, trying to figure out who I was. For me, divorce had always been unthinkable. But there I was, standing in the wreckage of what was, wondering what I was supposed to do next.

It felt as if a fire had burned through my life. Perhaps you feel that way too. Maybe for you the flames are still raging, consuming your trust, your dreams, your sense of security. Maybe it smoldered quietly for years, wearing you down until there was nothing left to save. Or perhaps you made choices you deeply regret, and now you're sifting through the ashes, asking if redemption is even possible. And where you are right now—this was never the plan.

Through my separation and divorce, I searched desperately for something—anything—to help me make

sense of what I was facing. At times I wondered if God had abandoned me, convinced that faithful Christians weren't supposed to go through this. I needed to know that I wasn't losing my mind, that I wasn't alone, and that God was still with me.

That's why I put these pages together—to offer what I couldn't find. I wanted a guide to help me navigate this unfamiliar path, to warn me of dangers, and to offer reassurance along the way. I'm hoping this book will serve in that way, as if a trusted friend were walking beside you. And I want you to know that whether your divorce was sudden or slow, whether you saw it coming or never imagined it would happen to you, whether it feels like rescue or ruin or a strange combination of the two, you will get through this.

Right now, healing may feel impossible. Joy, or even just stability, may feel out of reach because you're focusing on survival. Maybe you're not sure how you'll fit into this new life or if rebuilding is even possible. The pain and hopelessness may feel all too real. Perhaps you can relate to these words: "A man's spirit will endure sickness, but a crushed spirit who can bear?" (Proverbs 18:14). Or like Jeremiah, you've felt so overwhelmed that you've cried out, "My soul is bereft of peace; I have forgotten what happiness is; so I say, 'My endurance has perished; so has my hope from the LORD'" (Lamentations 3:17–18).

Those words captured what I couldn't manage to express at the time. And the poem below gives language to that ache too. The words aren't mine, but they could have been:

new normal.

*i don't think we talk enough about
how quiet the road gets. how long
the waiting feels. how lonely healing
can be. i don't think we talk enough
about how undone we become in the
valley of grief. or how enormously we
must stretch just to fit ourselves into
some kind of a new normal and dare
to call it life again. and i don't think
we talk enough about how we have no
other thing left but to gather up our
heavy limbs and carry on. because the
earth keeps on spinning. the sun keeps
on rising. and the days keep on bleeding,
one into the next, regardless of the
moment that made all the minutes inside
of our heart stand still.*

—ullie-kaye[1]

THE IMMEDIATE AFTERMATH

When my own marriage fell apart, the grief didn't hit all at once. It came in waves—some expected, others catching me off guard. The loss wasn't just relational; it was the unraveling of everything familiar. I woke up in a world that looked the same, but now I wasn't sure how to live in it.

Before we go on, let me share a bit of my story. I met my husband when I was 25, and we were married a year later. After nearly 18 years of marriage, he came home from a business trip and announced he was in love with

1 *Fires: Hardship, Grief and Perseverance* (Independently published, 2024), p. 112.

someone else and wanted to move on; our life together felt stifling.

I was stunned. I knew that he'd been distant for a while, but I had not foreseen this—never this. I later learned that they'd been involved for a year, and the fact that I hadn't suspected anything made me feel foolish on top of everything else. She lived in another state, and his extended work trips had been centered around seeing her.

After his announcement, everything changed. Our daughters, aged 10 and 13, were devastated as they struggled to make sense of what was happening. Weeks later, their dad moved 400 miles away, leaving me to parent alone while managing a neuromuscular disease that was steadily weakening my muscles. We were separated for three years—an excruciating season of uncertainty—before finally divorcing. Soon after, he married the woman he had left me for. I was relieved the waiting was over but gutted by all that had happened.

This wasn't the first time my world had fallen apart. Years earlier, I had buried my infant son, Paul, after a doctor's mistake led to his death at just two months old. His loss nearly crushed me. And now, I was facing another staggering reality—losing my marriage and the future I had once felt sure of.

In the first months after our separation, I remember shaking uncontrollably, wrapped in blankets, unable to get warm. I was in shock, terrified about the future, drowning in a sea of wordless emotions. Unanswerable questions filled my mind: Why wasn't I enough? How would the kids and I make it? Could I pull myself together enough to parent my daughters? What could I tell them—and what would I tell others? I felt afraid and angry, humiliated and helpless, bewildered and broken—all at once.

I've kept a journal for years, and during that season it became both a lifeline and a mirror—a place in which to wrestle with my thoughts and hold on to what I knew was true. Throughout this book, I'll share pieces of it—glimpses into those raw moments. One entry that stands out is from the time I ran into someone I hadn't seen in a while. I wrote:

> *"The other day, I ran into [an old acquaintance] at an event. He asked about [my ex], and I gave my usual answer: 'He's fine.' But something in me snapped, and before I could stop myself, I added, 'We're no longer together. He left me a few months ago.'*
>
> *"Dead silence. He didn't say a word. Just nodded, then slowly and deliberately turned away to another conversation. I know he felt awkward—he didn't know what to say. But his silence spoke volumes.*
>
> *"I kept talking to people, careful to avoid a few, grateful for the ones I didn't have to. But when the conversations ended, I walked out by myself and got into an empty car. Darkness was falling, and the isolation settled in. I had the radio on but turned it off. I needed silence—to feel the stillness, not fill it with noise."*

In those early days, even small interactions could leave me reeling. Grief consumed me, leaving me incapable of focusing on anything for more than a few seconds. Simple tasks like driving, making a grocery list, or answering texts became monumental challenges. I wondered how long it would take to feel normal again—or if I ever would.

I cried at the most inconvenient times—mid-conversation, in the car, standing in line at the store. Sometimes it was triggered by a song, sometimes by nothing at all. Other times I was too numb to cry, just

staring blankly, trying to remember what life had been before it unraveled.

HOW NOT TO TALK TO YOUR DOCTOR

One of the disorienting aspects of walking through divorce is that what consumes your thinking is just a detail (if even that) to the rest of the world. A few weeks after my divorce, I went to see a new doctor for back pain. It was just another appointment for him. But for me, everything felt different. Sitting in the waiting room, I filled out the usual forms, checking boxes that now felt foreign. Marital status: single, married, divorced... I hesitated. I didn't feel divorced. I didn't want that to be my identity. But after staring at it for far too long, I finally checked the box.

When the doctor walked in, he glanced at my chart for what felt like a few too many seconds. Naturally, I panicked. *He knows. He sees the box. He thinks I failed at marriage.* So I did the only thing that seemed sensible—I launched into an unsolicited explanation.

"I just want to say that I really valued my marriage," I blurted out. "I take commitment seriously. I wasn't planning on being divorced. I didn't want this, and I—"

The doctor raised an eyebrow and then looked back down at his notes. "I was just checking to see where your back hurts."

Right. That.

Note to self: doctors do not review your medical chart to assess your worthiness as a spouse. Next time, just check the box and move on.

Maybe you, too, have found yourself explaining your divorce to people who weren't even asking—justifying your story, proving your worth, making sure they know you're not "that kind" of divorced person. It's exhausting. Most have no idea of all you've been through. It's one

thing to be hurt by a stranger, but when it comes from the one who vowed to love you, the pain is sharper. They knew your hopes, your fears, your best and worst moments—yet they still chose to hurt you. If you're anything like me, you spent months, maybe years, making excuses, giving grace, holding on, only to painfully realize you were the only one fighting for your marriage.

Maybe now you feel lonelier than ever before. I did. I found it especially lonely walking into church by myself, feeling as if everyone saw a giant scarlet "D" stamped on my forehead. When people asked, "How are you?" I wasn't sure what they really wanted to hear. Should I pretend I was fine? Should I admit that I really wasn't? Either way, I felt unknown in a place that had once felt like home.

Friendships changed after my divorce. Some people were supportive, but others backed away. Maybe they didn't know what to say. Maybe they assumed I needed space. But what I needed was someone to sit with—not to fix me but simply to stay and listen.

Divorce carries layers of pain, with betrayal, shame, and loneliness often intertwined. But you'll notice that several times in this chapter I've talked about the grief of it. This layer, I find, isn't always acknowledged.

Divorced people don't get the same support as those who have been widowed. A friend once told me about two women in her neighborhood, both in their 30s, both pregnant. One was widowed when her husband died of cancer. The other was abandoned when her husband left her for someone else. The first woman was showered with meals, childcare, financial support, and a community that showed up for her. The second woman? She got awkward silence. Pitying looks at the grocery store. And then, nothing.

Both women had had their lives upended. Both faced a future they didn't choose. But one grief was met

with casseroles and comfort, the other with whispers and withdrawal—as if betrayal was easier to bear than death. But loss is loss. And just because it comes with a forsaking instead of a funeral doesn't mean it hurts us any less.

THE UNRAVELING AND THE WRESTLING

Divorce isn't just the loss of a relationship; it's the undoing of a covenant. On your wedding day, you stood before witnesses and promised unity: *for better, for worse, for richer, for poorer, in sickness and in health, till death do us part.* A divorce decree, in contrast, legally declares the marriage dissolved, listing the division of assets, custody agreements, and financial obligations, and restoring both parties to single status. The promises of love and permanence are undone in a few legal sentences, reducing what was once a shared life to a court order and some paperwork. It is the great undoing—the reversal of what was once sacred. The paperwork may be over, but the pain certainly isn't.

Now there are things to wrestle with that you never thought you'd have to.

For me, that meant wrestling with what divorce meant for my faith, my future, and my standing with God. I wasn't the first—the church has grappled with these same questions for centuries. Before my divorce, I hadn't spent much time thinking about what the Bible actually said about it, except for knowing that "God hates divorce." (Which was fine for me, because I wasn't going to be getting a divorce. Until I did.)

Now, as a divorced person or someone who is walking through that process, you may be wondering what God thinks about what has happened.

The church has long wrestled with what Scripture

teaches about divorce—how to fit together the places where the Bible speaks of it as contrary to God's will or sinful (Mark 10:1-9; Luke 16:18), as a reluctant concession (Deuteronomy 24:1-4; Matthew 19:8), as a necessary mercy (1 Corinthians 7:15), and as a breaking of a sacred covenant (Malachi 2:16; Matthew 5:32).

This is a complex and ongoing conversation that is beyond the scope of this book. In an appendix, I've included books and articles that reflect a range of biblical perspectives on the topic. Let me say this gently but clearly: I'm not encouraging anyone to leave a marriage without biblical grounds, nor am I discouraging someone whose spouse has deeply violated their vows from receiving the protection and freedom that Scripture offers. In this book, we're looking at how the gospel speaks to everyone—regardless of how they got to where they are. The gospel is for all of us, offering grace in our failures and hope for redemption, wherever we find ourselves.

It's important to note that while Scripture only explicitly mentions adultery and abandonment by a spouse as grounds for divorce, biblical ethics also calls us to ask: When does chronic abuse or addiction become a form of abandonment? At what point do these things violate the marriage covenant in the same way as adultery? As you may have discovered, these questions don't always have clear-cut answers. Because what constitutes abuse is widely debated, it's important to be clear about terms. "Abuse" can refer to a wide range of mistreatment—from controlling words to coercive behavior to physical violence—and the harm caused by such oppression can be devastating. However, not every situation labeled as abuse reflects a breaking of the marriage covenant. As biblical counselor Darby Strickland writes, "Labeling something as abuse when it is not will do damage ... to the people

involved and also to the women we encounter after them who truly are being abused."[2]

Mislabeling can cause significant harm—both when genuine abuse is ignored and when difficult or disappointing marriages are wrongly classified as abusive. That's why biblical counsel from trusted pastors, church leaders, or outside biblical counselors is so important. They can help discern whether someone is navigating the ordinary difficulties of marriage or facing abuse—and step in to offer support and advocacy when needed. (The resources in the appendix help readers understand the nature of domestic abuse and how the church can respond with wisdom and compassion.)

As the theologian Jim Newheiser says:

> *"It's best to look at spousal abuse as a particularly heinous form of marital neglect. In recent years, churches have explicitly recognized that we must take seriously all patterns of oppression and coercion, not just physical violence. As with the other grounds for divorce, we need discernment to recognize the difference between ordinary marital conflict and abuse."* [3]

And as you and I know, this is not just a theological discussion—it's personal. "Divorce is not simply a question to be answered but a journey to be walked," writes counselor Brad Hambrick. "Questions can be resolved quickly—journeys take time, even when you know the direction."[4] This is especially true for those

---

2 Darby Strickland, *Is It Abuse? A Biblical Guide to Identifying Domestic Abuse and Helping Victims* (P&R Publishing, 2020), p. 26.

3 Jim Newheiser, "What Does the Bible Teach About Divorce and Remarriage?" The Gospel Coalition, July 15, 2024; thegospelcoalition.org/article/bible-divorce-remarriage/ (accessed July 10, 2025).

4 Brad Hambrick, "Summit Small Group: Understanding Adultery, Abuse,

who are trying to make sense of divorce after betrayal or abuse. Being pro-marriage does not mean ignoring adultery or abuse. God cares deeply about the institution of marriage, but he also cares deeply about the individuals within it.

Like Newheiser, most pastors do not consider divorce sinful in cases of adultery, abuse, or abandonment. Yet, despite this, divorce often reshapes a person's relationship with the church. Nearly 47% of those who divorce leave their congregation,[5] and many struggle to find a new church they feel able to settle in. For some, the church becomes a place of comfort; for others, it becomes a source of shame, making an already painful season that was not their fault even worse. If that has been your experience, hear this: God sees you, and he does not condemn you. He does not stand on the side of the treacherous. He stands with the wounded. And he stands with you.

But if you're reading this knowing that you were the one who caused deep hurt, I want you to know this too: God's grace is not beyond your reach. Forgiveness is on offer. Repentance opens the door to redemption, and healing is still possible—even if you were the one who broke what was meant to last.

A FAITH SHAKEN

Divorce doesn't just shake your life—it often shakes your faith. Maybe you're struggling to pray. Maybe some days are okay, and on others you don't know where God is.

---

and Divorce"; bradhambrick.com/wp-content/uploads/2018/04/SummitSG_AdulteryAbuseDivorce_Handout.pdf (accessed April 12, 2025).

5 Bob Smietana, "Threat of Divorce Hard to Spot Among Churchgoing Couples," Lifeway Research, October 29, 2015; lifewayresearch.com/2015/10/29/threat-of-divorce-hard-to-spot-among-churchgoing-couples/ (accessed April 12, 2025).

Maybe you don't see the point of following God anymore at all. You trusted him, you believed in his goodness, and yet here you are, sifting through the ruins of a life you thought was secure.

I understand that. After my divorce, I didn't just grieve my marriage—I grieved the faith I thought I had. I had prayed for my husband, believed for change, begged God for restoration. But no matter how much I prayed, the outcome didn't change. What was the point of trusting God if he wasn't going to answer?

In the Old Testament book of Job, Job's friend Elihu captured what I was feeling when he intimated that Job felt this: "A man gains nothing when he becomes God's friend" (Job 34:9, CSB). Job didn't say those words, but I might as well have, because, in those first months, I wasn't sure what faith had given me except more pain.

Maybe you feel the same way. Maybe your faith in Jesus feels fragile and you're wondering if God even cares. I can assure you that God's love for you is deeper than you can comprehend. He knows all you've been through: all the tears you've cried and all the ways you've been wounded. He is for you, not against you, no matter how it feels at this moment. Though you may not sense his presence, in Jesus nothing can separate you from his love (Romans 8:31, 37-39).

These incredible promises are for those who know and trust Jesus—and if that's something you're unsure of, I'd encourage you to bring that question to him. He welcomes the weary and the searching.

If you have put your hope in him, the Lord will always be faithful. Like David, you can be confident that God has a plan and purpose for your life. The psalmist both declares and pleads, "The LORD will fulfill his purpose for me; your steadfast love, O LORD, endures forever. Do not forsake

the work of your hands" (Psalm 138:8). He clings to the truth of God's love while still asking for reassurance—and you can do the same.

The Hebrew word translated "steadfast love" here is *hesed*, a rich and layered term that speaks of God's loyal, enduring, faithful love and kindness. *Hesed* is a love that never gives up, that acts on our behalf, and that we can always count on. This love isn't based on our worthiness but on his covenant and character. Because of that, we can trust God to keep his promises—even when we fail.

Not only that, but God does work for the good of those who love him (Romans 8:28). Right now, you may not see how any good could come from this. And that's understandable. You don't need to rush to the part where everything feels better. Just know that God is present in this chapter of your life and will be in the next.

For a long time, I wrestled with God in my pain. But as the months passed, I realized something profound—my divorce hadn't been only the breaking of my heart; it had also been the making of my faith. Before my marriage ended, I loved God. I studied Scripture, taught Bible studies, and believed his promises. But after my ex left, I totally depended on Jesus. When everyone else walked out, he stayed. When I felt abandoned, he was near. When I had nothing left, he carried me. Looking back, I can see how God met me in those moments, even though I didn't always recognize it. In that same journal entry after running into that old acquaintance, I ended with this:

> *"It's in my emptiness that I meet God. My marriage had masked my need for him. I didn't need God to be my best friend—I already had one. I didn't need to give him my crushed hopes and dreams—they weren't that crushed anyway. But my aloneness has made me lean into God*

> *in a way that I couldn't have imagined. He is my best friend, my confidant and my counselor. And he will never abandon me."*

God's promises weren't just words on a page anymore; they were my lifeline. And somehow, in losing what I thought I couldn't live without, I found the one I truly couldn't live without.

BEFORE WE MOVE FORWARD

Right now, rebuilding might feel far off. That's completely understandable. My aim in this book isn't to offer a quick fix—it's to walk with you through this journey. Feeling whole again takes time, and I'm praying this book will help.

A few things as we get started:

- I write from my experience as a woman, which means you'll hear about things I did—like sobbing in the car, excessively snacking on dark chocolate, rationalizing retail therapy, and overanalyzing text messages with friends. If you're a man reading this, you may need to "translate" a few things—but the underlying truths are universal.
- Throughout the book, I refer to my former husband simply as "my ex." It's just the shorthand I'll be using.
- Take your time. These chapters build on each other, but if you need to skip ahead or reread certain sections, that's completely fine. Read in your own way and at your own pace.

Now, let's talk about what it looks like to rebuild.

REBUILDING AND MOVING FORWARD

Divorce may feel like an ending, and it is—but it is not the end of you. Moving forward doesn't mean erasing

the past; it means embracing what's ahead without letting the past define you. Maybe you don't know who you are outside of your marriage. Maybe rebuilding—finances, parenting, friendships, faith—feels impossible. Or maybe you're just exhausted from trying to hold it all together. That's okay.

Growth is slow, and it's not a straight line. On some days, you'll feel stronger. On other days, it'll seem like you're back at square one. So keep track of your small victories—because you're making progress even when it doesn't feel like it. Over the page, you'll find a tracking grid. Each week, try to rate how you're doing in these areas on a 1-to-4 scale—1 being struggling, 4 being doing well.

Don't overthink it—just place a check-mark where you land each week. If you want to go a little deeper, write a single word to describe why you put the check-mark there: "exhausted," "hopeful," "frustrated," "stronger," or whatever. Over time, you might notice small but real changes. If you'd like a printable version of this tracker, you can download one at thegoodbook.com/never-the-plan-tracker. It's adapted from DivorceCare, though I've simplified it here.[6] It's simply a way to mark where you are—without any pressure to be moving upward—and to acknowledge the steps of the journey.

And if you don't see movement right away, that's normal too. On some days, your biggest victory might just be getting out of bed and acting like a semifunctional human. If all you managed today was putting on something resembling real clothes and eating a meal that didn't come from a crumpled takeout bag, that's still something. Technically, that counts as self-care. Go ahead and check "managing" under Physical Health—and maybe even write down what you ate, just to make it official.

---

6 *DivorceCare* (Church Initiative, 2020), p. 8.

	EMOTIONAL WELL-BEING	PHYSICAL HEALTH	CLOSENESS TO GOD	FRIENDSHIPS, COMMUNITY	SENSE OF HOPE
1					
2					
3					
4					

NOT THE END

You may not feel it yet, but this is not the end of your story. Divorce doesn't get the last word. You can be better, not bitter. Free, not chained. Healing is possible. It won't happen overnight, but it can happen.

And in the meantime? You might break down in public, devour a pint of ice cream (or an entire rack of ribs), or dramatically toss old love letters (or that hoodie they conveniently left behind) into the trash or the bonfire. This season may have broken pieces of your life, but it has not broken you. One day, without realizing it, you'll step into a new chapter—not because the pain has disappeared but because you have kept walking forward. You can't change the past, but your future is ahead of you. And it's worth stepping into.

CHAPTER 2

TEARS, FEARS, AND THE TENDERNESS OF GOD

I remember going to the grocery store after my marriage dissolved. I wandered aimlessly, unable to find the few items I'd gone in for. After staring for ten minutes at the boxed brownies, I noticed my neighbor and ducked into the next aisle to avoid her. I couldn't even begin to make conversation. I left the store empty-handed, got into my minivan, and collapsed into tears. How could this be my life? Would I ever feel normal again? Would I ever stop crying? All I knew was that I was living a nightmare.

Everything exhausted me—physically, emotionally, and mentally. I could echo Job's words: "For the thing I feared has overtaken me, and what I dreaded has happened to me. I cannot relax or be calm; I have no rest, for turmoil has come" (Job 3:25-26, CSB). Fear. Dread. Tension. Unrest. Turmoil. Those words summed up my life.

At the time I felt weak and inadequate, wishing I was stronger and more courageous. But now, looking back, I realize that even getting up every morning was brave.

Right now you are also being brave. Yes, really—even

if you don't feel like it. It takes courage to even open the pages of this book and want to walk forward. It's easier to numb your pain or try to forget it rather than to face the jumbled emotions inside you.

Few people who walk through a divorce do so unwounded. Some of my deepest wounds came from the callousness of my ex-husband's words and actions. I wrote this in my journal after he left:

> *"The words are what sting. They come back to me when I close my eyes, and even when I try to push them away. They hiss, 'You don't count. You're not good enough. And you don't matter enough for me to ease your pain. I may have betrayed you and lied to you and abandoned you, but that's not all. I need you to understand that it wasn't my fault—it's not a problem with me—it's a problem with you. So don't take any comfort in believing that I once loved you deeply and truly, that I hated hurting you. No, I never had passion for you, and I'll never bring you flowers. You just aren't worth it.'"*

There's nothing quite like rereading old journals to dredge up painful memories. I've made a note to myself not to do that again just before going to a party.

My ex didn't actually say most of what I wrote—but it's what I took away. I didn't matter. I'd given him my hopes and dreams, I'd trusted him to protect me and love me, and now I felt foolish, questioning what was real in my marriage. How could we have begun with such promise and ended with such brokenness?

You may relate to my journal entry, or your emotions after divorce may be completely different. Whatever you're feeling, don't ignore it, hoping it will magically disappear. Instead, I encourage you to pay attention—your emotions are God-given signposts to help you understand yourself.

So here is your invitation to welcome every emotion that arises. Emotions themselves aren't good or bad—they're simply natural responses to what's happening in and around you. Be curious about what's behind them. Don't push them away or rush past them, because that only gives them more power. Ignoring your emotions isn't spiritual—it short-circuits healing and can keep you from deeper intimacy with God.

Naming your emotions is one thing, but processing them is another. So how do you begin to work through grief, especially when you don't know when it will show up?

GIVING VOICE TO YOUR FEELINGS

My emotions kept ambushing me. They would pop up unpredictably and at the most unwelcome times. One moment I felt strong; the next I was in tears—in the grocery store, at a movie, driving past familiar places. Memories, both beautiful and painful, surfaced in the most ordinary moments, often when I least expected them. To process them, alongside journaling daily I made a scrapbook, filling it with song lyrics, photos, emails, and thoughts—capturing whatever I was feeling in the moment. On one page, I wrote in large letters...

> *"Sometimes I feel... betrayed, unloved, incompetent, inadequate, rejected, angry, foolish, helpless, worthless, lonely, stupid, flawed, unwanted, failure, inconsequential, uncertain, discouraged, and afraid."*

Writing those words gave me an odd sense of release—just naming them took away some of their weight.

So let me encourage you to take a moment to name what's stirring in you right now. If you feel able to, jot down a few words in the margin or on your phone. Be honest. The more you name your emotions, the better you'll understand

yourself and be able to process what's happening. Remember, emotions are signposts, pointing to deeper realities. Paying attention to them can be the difference between staying stuck and moving toward healing.

For the remainder of the chapter, I'm going to walk through the emotions I felt in my grief and how I dealt with them (or how I *wish* I'd dealt with them). I had to remember that my emotions didn't define who I was, but they were how I felt. You may feel all of these at some point, or just a few. Some might hit you in waves; others might linger. It's all part of the process.

We'll start with shock and confusion—the emotions that tend to accompany the immediate disorientation that comes with divorce—followed by a brief look at anger, since I'll explore it more fully in other chapters. Then we'll move into shame and doubt, which creep in as we question ourselves and our faith, and then sadness and depression, which often arise as the weight of loss begins to settle. Many people also experience a complicated mix of relief and grief over unresolved, undefined losses. We'll spend the most time on fear, since it shapes so much of the journey forward. And finally, we'll process it all with the Lord through lament—an invitation to bring every emotion, unfiltered, to him.

SHOCK AND CONFUSION

In the first days after my separation, I felt as if I was moving through a fog. Nothing seemed real. I went through the motions, but underneath I was numb—too disoriented to process what had happened. Then, when the shock started to wear off, confusion took its place.

I remember writing in my journal, *Who am I?* and *What is true?* I didn't know who I was anymore or what was real. It took time to think clearly, to stop questioning

myself, and to see that my identity wasn't tied to being married.

We all wrestle with confusion after loss. Roles shift, responsibilities grow, and the life we knew feels unfamiliar. It's natural to question everything—your judgment, your past, even your future. You may have seen this coming for a long time, or you may still be in shock. Either way, you might feel lost, unsure of who you are or where you belong. Let your confusion be a catalyst—not of fear but for moving you to find clarity.

ANGER

Though I wasn't slow to get angry, I was slow to admit it to myself because I wanted to look perfect. While I internally erupted, I kept my emotions well hidden and then saw them pop up in other, more insidious ways. When I finally started acknowledging and confessing my hidden resentment and asking God for help, my anger became constructive. It propelled me forward and gave me courage to name what was unjust and to set healthy boundaries.

We often see anger as something to completely get rid of, but it isn't inherently sinful. It all depends on how we handle it. God is slow to anger, and we are called to be the same.

You may feel anger after divorce—at your spouse, yourself, even God. Instead of burying it, bring it to God. Anger can either consume you or move you toward healing. How you process it can make all the difference.

SHAME

I felt so much shame after my separation and divorce. While we all have regrets about what we did and didn't do, I was sure that my husband's rejection was about

my inadequacies. His leaving convinced me that I wasn't worth loving, pursuing, or sharing his life with.

I remember driving in the car, feeling horrible about myself, and wondering what would bring my husband back, when the words "It's not about you" popped into my mind. I hadn't even stopped to consider that possibility. Immediately, my mind stopped swirling, my heart stopped racing, and an unfamiliar sense of calm settled over me. I felt the Lord reassuring me that I wasn't responsible for my husband's actions. What happened wasn't about me. And that realization freed me from berating myself and trying to fix everything on my own.

We often assume that if someone rejects us, it must be because we weren't enough. Shame tells us that we must be the problem. But you do not need to feel shame for what you were not responsible for. I hope you realize that what happened to you isn't a reflection of your worth. You are a beloved child of God, infinitely valuable. So don't let your ex's behavior define you. You are not unlovable. You are not unworthy. You are deeply loved by the one who will never leave you.

While the shame of my husband's rejection once consumed me, when that dissipated, it was only for a new sense of shame to take its place. I was ashamed that I had been so trusting, not recognizing what was happening but believing what my ex told me. I felt foolish and gullible, especially when a friend commented, "I'm sure you suspected something, right?" No, I actually didn't. Or maybe in hindsight I ignored the little signs because I was certain of my husband's character, or perhaps I was afraid to face what felt like my worst fears.

If that's the kind of shame that weighs on you, I encourage you to bring that to the Lord as well. Don't let

other people's opinions about what you should have seen or done make you feel judged or unworthy. God knows your heart and all your insecurities, fears and doubts, so pour them all out to him.

DOUBT

While I am confident of God's care now, when my marriage first fell apart so did my trust in God's love. I questioned everything, even shouting my doubts to God. So many nights, I sobbed into my pillow, "God, why do you hate me? Don't you even care?" I even screamed those words in front of my pastor as I was trying to make sense of why all this had happened.

God's answer came tenderly through Scripture. While God didn't give me a reason, he did reassure me of his love. I ended up reading Isaiah 54 almost every day, clinging to God's promises

For the mountains may depart
and the hills be removed,
but my steadfast love shall not depart from you.
(Isaiah 54:10)

Even when I felt storm-tossed and abandoned, God saw me. He knew my sorrow. None of my pain would be wasted.

Today your trust in God may feel fragile. Perhaps you trusted he'd turn your situation around, but instead your circumstances got worse. Maybe you wonder whether you even want to trust God again. And maybe those doubts are even intensifying your sadness.

SADNESS AND DEPRESSION

Those tearful nights kept me awake, flooded with questions and emotion that swirled around me. Again, I

could identify with Job: "When I lie down I think, 'When will I get up?' But the evening drags on endlessly, and I toss and turn until dawn" (Job 7:4, CSB). My tears felt as if they were my only food (Psalm 42:3), as everything else felt tasteless. Life was gray, days blurred together, and I felt disconnected from my body and my mind.

We all experience sadness in grief, but sometimes it lingers and deepens into depression. Depression can feel like carrying a heavy weight, making every decision and every step a struggle. Some of us retreat, crawling into bed and sleeping to escape while others stay awake all night. Even faithful people in Scripture—David, Jeremiah, Elijah, and Job—felt hopeless at times. When we're worn out, afraid, and unsure of the future, it's hard to believe we'll ever see good again.

You may feel that sadness is a constant presence in your life. If so, please know you're not alone and this won't last forever. While depression is a normal part of grief, it can become dangerous. If you're having suicidal thoughts or struggling to care for yourself or your family, reach out to someone you trust—a friend, pastor, counselor, physician, or family member. There's no shame in seeking help. Prayer, medicine, exercise, and talking through your feelings can all be part of healing. In a later chapter, I'll share more ways to cope, but for now, hold on to this: no matter how deep the darkness feels, it won't always be this way.

RELIEF

When my ex first left, I didn't feel relief. I was shocked and hurt. I grieved, questioned, and held on to what had been. But after my divorce was finalized, I slowly began to see that my divorce was part of God's best for me, and my husband's rejection was God's protection.

We don't always recognize relief when it comes. For some, it's the freedom of finally feeling safe—no longer walking on eggshells or bracing for violence. For others, it's the clarity of knowing where things stand after years of uncertainty. You may not feel relief yet. You may still long for what was. But in time, you may see that God was rescuing you in ways you never expected.

UNDEFINED GRIEF

Even after I started feeling relief, I still felt the sting of my ongoing and complicated losses. I couldn't put them on a shelf and find closure. I was mourning what I had lost, what I had once hoped for, and what would never be.

I felt a mixture of disbelief and foolishness at the fact that the person I had shared my dreams with, who knew my heart better than anyone else, wasn't for me anymore. I remember sitting at a basketball game on the other side of the gym from my ex, tears slowly rolling down my cheeks. It wasn't supposed to be like this. We should have been cheering together, rather than me glancing over at him, remembering how it once was. There were so many unknowns and uncertainties, and I didn't know how to process them all.

I missed the everyday moments that my husband and I had spent together: simple interactions like telling him the details of my day, eating leftovers with someone who wouldn't complain, or watching TV with someone who agreed that yelling at the screen actually helped. My children shared none of these habits.

Divorce brings ambiguous loss, a term used to describe losses that are unclear, unresolved, and lack closure. It's grieving not just what's gone but what remains in a different, often painful form. Maybe you're mourning the fact that your kids won't have an intact family. Or that

your friendships will change. Or that celebrations like graduations or weddings, or family milestones like having grandchildren, will have awkwardness intertwined with happiness. Your dreams for the future are now different, or maybe you're afraid to dream at all.

FEAR

Not only had my dreams been shattered when my marriage dissolved, but I never thought I'd face so many new fears. My greatest concern was for my daughters as I wondered how our divorce would impact them, both in the short- and long-term. I was afraid of the daily responsibilities my husband had always handled: home maintenance, paying bills, figuring out which smoke detector was going off at 3 a.m. And I was terrified that I'd find a spider lurking in a corner, knowing I would need to drown it with the can of bug spray I'd stored in every room (seriously).

I realized my fear was forward-facing, meaning it was connected to threats of what might happen more than what was happening. I wanted control, believing that if I managed every variable I could guarantee the outcome I wanted. But instead of feeling secure, I became anxious, as if I was playing a never-ending game of whack-a-mole. Just as I tackled one problem, another popped up.

Then I rediscovered the "Serenity Prayer," and began praying it every morning:

> *"God,*
> *Grant me the serenity to accept the things I cannot change,*
> *The courage to change the things I can,*
> *And the wisdom to know the difference."*

That prayer became my surrender to God—a reminder

that I didn't have to figure everything out on my own. With that, I'd often pray, "I feel powerless against everything that is coming against me. I don't know what to do, but my eyes are on you" (2 Chronicles 20:12).

HOW TO FACE FEAR

You may feel paralyzed by uncertainty, unsure of how to move forward. If that's where you are, here are three steps to begin to do that:

1. *Name your fears.* Fear thrives in the dark, but when you bring it into the light, it starts to lose its grip. Write down what you're dreading—both the small, daily worries and the life-altering ones that make your heart sink.
2. *Remember that Jesus is with you.* A friend once asked me, "Where is Jesus in your fears?" and then insisted I picture Jesus with me. That simple exercise brought me tremendous peace, and I think it might surprise you with the deep comfort it brings.
3. *Surrender what you can't control.* Pray the Serenity Prayer or meditate on a verse that reminds you of God's faithfulness. You don't have to figure everything out. Trust that he will lead you through.

EVEN IF, NOT WHAT IF

I remember sitting at a retreat center after my divorce, feeling overwhelmed by fear and disappointment. As I poured out my fears, God met me in an unmistakable way as his presence surrounded me. In an article I wrote about that day, I said:

> *"God reminded me that I have something far better than a reassurance that my dreaded "what ifs" won't happen. I have the assurance that* ***even if*** *they do happen, he will be there in the midst of them. He will carry me. He will comfort me. He will tenderly care for me. God doesn't promise us a trouble-free life. But he does promise that he will be there in the midst of our sorrows."* [7]

Even if. Those two simple words have taken the fear out of life. Replacing "what if" with "even if" is one of the most liberating exchanges we can ever make. We trade our irrational fears of an uncertain future for the loving assurance of our unchanging God.

That day I realized that while God wasn't protecting me from trouble, he was protecting me *in* trouble. None of his promises had failed. Nothing could ever separate me from his love (Romans 8:36-39). Nothing was out of his control. While I didn't know what tomorrow would bring, God did. He knew what was around the corner and would give me all I needed to face it when I got there.

A PRAYER FOR YOU

Yet even when you know those truths, fear may still grip you. When it does, fill your mind with reminders of who God is. One of the verses that steadied me was...

Fear not, for I am with you;
be not dismayed, for I am your God;
I will strengthen you, I will help you,
I will uphold you with my righteous right hand.
(Isaiah 41:10)

---

7 Vaneetha Rendall Risner, "What If the Worst Happens?" Desiring God, September 15, 2014; desiringgod.org/articles/what-if-the-worst-happens (accessed April 12, 2025).

Maybe you need that reminder today. Maybe you need to see those words in multiple places—in your car, on your bathroom mirror, on notecards tucked in places where you'll notice them. A friend of mine wrote out Scriptures she wanted to hold on to, read them aloud each day, and put them everywhere I just mentioned, reminding herself that God's promises were truer than her circumstances.

And that is my prayer for you: that in the midst of your fear and uncertainty, you would experience the steady presence of God: that his words would strengthen you, his love would carry you, and his peace would hold you fast.

LAMENT: AN INVITATION TO HONESTY

Even though I held on to God's promises, sometimes I couldn't even put words to my grief. It was then that I sat with God in silence, trusting that he knew exactly what I was feeling. I leaned on the Holy Spirit, who intercedes in our weakness with groanings too deep for words (Romans 8:26). I learned that sometimes the deepest prayers aren't spoken—they're simply groaned.

And that's where lament begins.

I once thought I could only bring joy, thankfulness, and praise to God. But Scripture tells a different story. Men and women throughout the Bible trusted God enough to bring him their pain, disappointment, and even frustration. They didn't hide behind pious words—they poured out their raw, unfiltered emotions. And God welcomed their honesty.

Lament is the language of grief for the believer. It's telling God about our sadness, confusion, and anger as they are, trusting that he can hold them. It's wrestling with him, protesting about what feels unfair, expressing sorrow and outrage, all while choosing to engage with him rather than turning away.

When I read laments in Scripture, I saw that God doesn't tell us to push down our grief and pretend everything is fine. Instead, the Bible is full of raw, unfiltered cries:

How long, O LORD? Will you forget me forever? (Psalm 13:1)

You have wrapped yourself with a cloud so that no prayer can pass through. (Lamentations 3:44)

My God, my God, why have you forsaken me? (Psalm 22:1, a cry echoed by Jesus on the cross)

Even Jesus lamented. Hebrews 5:7 tells us, "During his earthly life, he offered prayers and appeals with loud cries and tears to the one who was able to save him from death" (CSB). If Jesus cried out to God in suffering, so can we.

Lament isn't grumbling. It's not complaining *about* God to others—it's bringing our pain *to* him, believing he cares. It's a form of worship: a bold declaration that even in our darkest moments, we are choosing to engage with God rather than turn away.

HOW TO LAMENT

If lament feels unnatural to you, you're not alone. The church often praises those who grieve "cheerfully," equating outward composure with deep faith. But Scripture teaches that bringing our sorrow to God *is* an act of faith. There's no right way to lament—just be honest with God. He longs to hear your heart, even when it feels messy and broken.

If you've never lamented, start small. Pray out loud, journal your thoughts, or write your own psalm. If you don't know where to start, Mark Vroegop offers a simple framework based on the Psalms:[8]

8 Mark Vroegop, "Dare to Hope in God: How to Lament Well," Desiring

1. *Turn to God:* Begin by addressing God directly.
2. *State your complaint:* Be honest about your pain, questions, and frustrations.
3. *Ask for help:* Tell God what you need, both the small and the significant.
4. *Choose to trust:* Even in your grief, affirm your faith in his goodness.

Lament takes wild trust. For me, it took the form of journaling; of writing down my every unfiltered emotion. After my ex left, my sister once skimmed what I'd journaled and was shocked—she still affectionately calls it my "scream journal." Later, she told me she had never trusted God enough to bring such honest emotions to him before. Through that practice, I learned that God wanted me to bring him everything. And as I look back, I see God's faithfulness on every page of that "scream journal." Rather than pushing God away, my laments drew me closer. They intensified my love for Jesus, showing me that I was fully seen, known, and loved by him.

Right now your grief may feel exhausting and unpredictable, but please know that God isn't standing far off, indifferent to your pain. He is breathtakingly near. He cares about every detail. He is lavishing his love on you. More than anyone on earth, God knows how hard this is. And he is right beside you.

Grief will not have the final say. Healing will come, not in an instant but step by step. Even though everything around you may look black, be assured that light is coming, and it will obliterate the darkness.

God, April 6, 2019; desiringgod.org/articles/dare-to-hope-in-god (accessed April 12, 2025).

CHAPTER 3

LETTING GO WITHOUT GIVING IN

As I read through my old journals, I was transported back to the first days of my separation. Those were days when I felt bewildered: days when I wondered what was wrong with me—days when I heard my ex confirm my worst fears, their impact on me apparently irrelevant to him. "I really don't know why I married you—we never had that spark" and "I love her now, and I don't love you anymore" and "I'm so much happier now."

Looking back, I don't know how I made it through those impossibly hard days.

I hoped counseling would change my husband's mind. I hoped that he'd come back to me, plead for my forgiveness, and tell me how much he loved me. But in one of those counseling sessions he declared, "I might consider coming back to our family even though I don't want to. I know it's the right thing. But don't ever expect me to win you back with wine and roses."

Those words brought stunning clarity. And I kept replaying them. I realized that while I had been clinging to hope, he had moved on.

I don't know what your story is, but I'm guessing you've dealt with pain and rejection. Your ex is probably not the person you once thought they were, and now you're wondering if they ever were that person. Whether this was the outcome you wanted or not, now you're faced with the challenge of healing and moving on. But how do you do that? The best way to start is by detaching.

DETACHING

Naturally I was curious about my ex-husband's new life. Who was this other-worldly goddess who brought a spark, love, and happiness wherever she went? Besides wondering about her, I had other questions too. Had my ex settled into his new life, was he as happy as he claimed, and did he ever regret leaving me? My interest seemed harmless; what I didn't know was that it was keeping me attached to him.

Detaching is challenging. Whatever the reason for your divorce, you might be tempted to keep tabs on your ex-spouse by following them on social media or asking mutual friends what they're doing. But if you do, you'll soon discover that the answers will inevitably lead to more questions—questions that will keep you emotionally tied to your ex. So here is my advice: resist the urge to figure out how they're spending their money, where they're vacationing, and why all your mutual friends haven't unfollowed them yet.

FORGIVING: LETTING GO OF BITTERNESS

As we talk about detaching, we also need to talk about forgiveness.

You may want to stop reading right now, or to hurl this book against the wall. Even the idea of forgiveness may feel unreasonable or unthinkable given what's happened. A

few months after my ex left, I literally threw the book I was reading across the room when it mentioned forgiveness. I felt irate and misunderstood. I didn't understand how I could forgive what had happened. So please know that I'm not trying to guilt you into anything, but rather I'm just asking you to bring this to God.

What changed my mind was realizing that unforgiveness was keeping me attached to my ex. It wasn't only my interest in his activities that kept me connected to him; it was also my continual mental rehearsal of how I'd been wronged, replaying the unkind things that he'd said. I thought about it constantly—standing in line at the grocery store, waiting at the doctor's office, and even before falling asleep every night. I fantasized about his life falling apart; I wanted to make him suffer as much as he'd made me suffer. Or at least I wanted him to suffer a little. That didn't seem wrong at all—it felt natural and understandable. I wasn't actively doing anything to hurt my ex, so what was the harm in it? But this preoccupation kept him at the forefront of my thoughts, and I realized I was imprisoned by it. The only way I could be free was to forgive.

But I wasn't sure if I could forgive, for two reasons. First, I just didn't want to do it. Second, I wasn't sure what it meant. So let me define what I mean by forgiveness here: in this book, when I speak of forgiveness I mean refusing to hold on to bitterness and voluntarily letting go of the right to hurt someone for hurting you. It's acknowledging that you've been wronged but choosing not to take revenge on the one who has hurt you. I don't see forgiveness as being dependent on the other person at all. They don't need to be sorry or even acknowledge what they've done. And you don't need to let them know you've forgiven them right away, because forgiveness is primarily between you and God.

WHAT FORGIVENESS IS *NOT*

So that's what forgiveness is—but it's just as important to know what forgiveness is not. Forgiveness is not overlooking what your ex did or minimizing what happened. It requires honestly facing the callous, cruel, or even horrific ways we've been treated without making any excuses for them. Christ needed to forgive our sin because we could never make up for it, so forgiving someone doesn't diminish the seriousness of what they did.

Forgiveness is also not the same as reconciliation. While forgiveness isn't dependent on the other person's attitude, reconciliation certainly is. The Lord doesn't tell us to reconcile without repentance. Repentance is not just mumbling, "I'm sorry." In repentance, someone first admits that what they did was wrong without blame-shifting. They humbly accept the consequences of their actions, change direction, and make God-honoring choices. It's what we see from Zacchaeus the tax collector in Luke 19 as he promised to restore fourfold to anyone he had defrauded. Without repentance, you don't need to restore trust or invite someone who has hurt you back into a relationship.

So if your ex apologizes but minimizes their sin or won't take responsibility for their actions, don't assume they're repentant. False repentance may sound like "I already said I was sorry. What more do you want from me?" or "Why are you still making such a big deal about this? Why can't you just accept what happened and move on?" No, repentance has fruit (Matthew 3:8): fruit that is clearly visible and life-giving—fruit that will be evident to you and to others who know your ex, including your family and mutual friends.

Finally, forgiveness is not saying that someone won't experience consequences for what happened. You may

need to pursue legal action against your spouse for financial support or for not fulfilling their part of the agreement, or you may need to file criminal charges if appropriate. But when you forgive, you are not making them repay you for their sinful actions. You are leaving those consequences to God, who promises, "Vengeance is mine. I will repay" (Romans 12:19). The Lord alone can bring real justice, and to forgive is to leave it with him.

WHY FORGIVE?

Defining forgiveness is all well and good, but still... why should you do it? Why voluntarily give up your right to revenge or to nurse a grudge? Here are three key reasons:

1. God calls us to forgive.

2. Forgiveness is essential for our healing.

3. If we don't forgive, we'll hurt the people around us.

I once thought forgiveness was optional—a nice thing to do if I felt like it. Not surprisingly, I never felt like it. I thought it was one of those "suggestion" commands, like giving sacrificially.[9] But in the Lord's prayer, Jesus tells us to ask for God's forgiveness as we have forgiven others. Then he says, "For if you forgive others their offenses, your heavenly Father will forgive you as well. But if you don't forgive others, your Father will not forgive your offenses" (Matthew 6:14-15, CSB). When I first focused on that idea, I was taken aback. It only started to become easier when I realized that forgiveness isn't primarily a transaction between me and the person who hurt me—it's an act of obedience between me and God. Jesus

---

9 I just want to clarify that there are no suggestion commands. I thought you'd recognize my sarcasm, but my editor wasn't so sure. Hence this footnote.

understands what forgiveness costs. He was betrayed, mocked, abandoned, and murdered so he could forgive our sins. When I was struggling with forgiveness, a friend offered these helpful words: "Forgiveness feels impossibly hard. But we are never as much like Christ as when we are willing to suffer for the sins of others."

People who can't forgive can't heal. I've seen that firsthand, and you probably have too. I've met divorced people who were still hardened by their resentment, even years later. They were anxious to offer even minor details about how they'd been wronged as if it all happened yesterday. Remembering those encounters made me want a different outcome for myself. I didn't want anger to grip me. I didn't want bitterness to define me. I didn't want to stay stuck in the past. I wanted to stop replaying the tape of how I'd been wronged because it was only hurting me. And the only way to stop the tape was to forgive. I agree with the often-quoted statement, "Resentment is like swallowing poison and hoping someone else will die." It sounds crazy, but that is what we all do. Forgiveness can remove the poison from our hands—it really is for our good.

You may think that nursing bitterness impacts only you. But it doesn't. Bitterness impacts everyone around us—the hardness in our eyes and the edge in our voice are unmistakable. We don't just hold on to bitterness; it holds on to us. As bitterness takes root, it produces poisonous fruit. This is why Hebrews 12:15 exhorts us, "See to it that no one fails to obtain the grace of God; that no 'root of bitterness' springs up and causes trouble, and by it many become defiled." Bitterness springs up quickly and causes trouble for everyone it touches. Over time, friends may back away from us, not wanting to be poisoned by our negativity—or they may be drawn into it, damaging

themselves. The greatest impact of our bitterness will be on our children, who must live under the weight of our simmering anger.

Left unchecked, bitterness will destroy our lives. Perhaps one of the most vivid examples of this is in the Charles Dickens novel *Great Expectations*. Miss Havisham was jilted at the altar as a young woman. Ever since that day, her mind and even her clocks have been set to the exact moment when she discovered her fiancé's deception. She lives in her disintegrating wedding dress, the cob-webbed dining table still set for the reception, the cake covered in fungus, largely eaten away by beetles and spiders. As she points to the horrifying decay, she remarks:

> *"It and I have worn away together. The mice have gnawed at it, and sharper teeth than teeth of mice have gnawed at me ... When the ruin is complete ... they [will] lay me dead in my bride's dress on the bride's table—which shall be done, and which will be the finished curse upon him."* [10]

The tragedy is that the curse was only on one person, and it wasn't her ex-fiancé. He had long forgotten her—though she somehow believed she was punishing him. It was she who suffered, imprisoned by her bitterness, the sharp teeth of unforgiveness gnawing away at her.

I wonder what Miss Havisham's life would have looked like if she had forgiven her fiancé months after he jilted her. What a different life she'd have had—far freer and far happier. That's why forgiveness matters. It matters for *your* life and *your* future. And it matters because it will draw you closer to the Lord on this difficult road you are walking.

---

10 Charles Dickens, *Great Expectations* (Penguin Classics, 2002), p. 98.

HOW DO WE FORGIVE?

Knowing that I needed to forgive and terrified by how bitterness had destroyed others, I begged God to remove my bitterness and help me forgive. But it still wasn't easy.

Honestly, the first step of forgiveness felt like death. I didn't want to do it. In fact, I never *want* to do it. What I want is to hold on to my right to be angry. I began by praying, "Lord, I don't want to forgive, but could you make me even *want to* want to forgive? You've forgiven all my sins, and I know anything I forgive others is small by comparison. But I can't do this without you. Please help me."

I prayed that daily, and it still took a while for me to even want to forgive. I knew I needed to be ready, so I kept bringing my heart and emotions to God. Before I could forgive, I needed space to process what had happened.

I caution against forgiving too quickly, especially if you don't really understand what you are forgiving. Linda MacDonald, a Christian therapist who walked through betrayal and divorce herself, writes:

> *"Don't let well-meaning Christian friends rush you into this process. First, you must take inventory of your grief, identify the debts, name the injuries, and assign proper responsibility for the wrongs committed against you. We must name our injuries clearly and truthfully."*

She goes on to ask:

> *"Have you been emotionally honest about how hurt and angry you are over your spouse's disloyalty and forsaking your marriage? Are you trying too hard to be brave? Have you given full vent to your feelings without trying to censor yourself to appear cool-headed, above the fray, or super spiritual?"*[11]

---

11 Linda J. MacDonald, *Redeeming the Post-Affair Divorce* (Healing Counsel Press: 2025), p. 363, 378

I encourage you to work through those issues and questions, without feeling pressure to "forgive and just move on."

My own process began by naming all that had happened—the betrayal, the unkind words, the lies, and the secrets. I detailed the impact of the separation and divorce on my life and the lives of those around me—my daughters, our extended family, the church, and even our community. I kept a small journal with me and furiously scribbled in it for weeks. I recorded what I'd lost, how I was struggling, and the implications for my future, interwoven with my rage, disappointment, and pain. Nothing was off-limits. I needed to know what I was letting go of, so I asked God to bring every detail to mind. And I wrote and I wrote until there was nothing more to write.

Then I reread all of it and brought it to God. I asked him to help me forgive. Then I explicitly declared my forgiveness, releasing to God my right to revenge. It began with that decision, but it was an ongoing process: a process that spanned years, because new offenses would continually come up and painful memories would resurface. When they did, I'd have to intentionally quit rehearsing what happened and release it to God.

This journey of forgiveness drew me to God in breathtaking ways. I realized that holding on to bitterness had created a barrier between me and God, though I didn't know at the time what was blocking me. When I was able to forgive, I felt incredible joy and release. When you forgive, you'll understand God's love and power in ways you've never experienced. As you surrender to him, those wounds you've suffered will connect you more deeply with Christ, the vine, and his life will flow through you (John 15:1-11). Only the Lord can enable you to forgive, and when you do, you'll be amazed at the freedom you feel.

I don't know where you are in your journey of forgiveness. Perhaps the wound is still too fresh, and you need time to process all that's happened. Maybe you've been holding on to bitterness, and it has hardened you. You may feel entitled to stay angry. Yet the longer you hold on to the pain, the harder it is to let it go. So I encourage you to ask God what to do next. He will show you.

THE POWER OF FORGIVENESS

In the account of the life of Joseph in Genesis 37 – 50, we see the power of forgiveness. Joseph was the favored son of Jacob, and his brothers despised him for that. They wanted to murder him, callously discussing their options over lunch even as Joseph was begging for his life. But when traveling traders passed by, Joseph's brothers impulsively sold him as a slave.

That is an almost unimaginable betrayal at the hands of your own family. Joseph could easily have held on to the pain of that betrayal, nursing his bitterness. But he didn't. Years later, when he rose to power in Pharaoh's house, he named his firstborn son Manasseh, based on the Hebrew word "making to forget." He explained, "God has made me forget all my hardship and all my father's house" (Genesis 41:51). How could Joseph forget all his hardship and how cruel his brothers cruel had been? He could forget because he'd chosen years before not to rehearse what they had done. Their actions weren't erased from his memory, but as he chose not to remember their cruelty, his brothers' betrayal had no power over him.

The next time Joseph saw his brothers, they came to ask for a favor, unaware of who he was. This would have been the perfect opportunity to exact revenge, but Joseph didn't take it. He forgave his brothers. Even years later, they could not believe it! But as Joseph put it, "As for you,

you meant evil against me, but God meant it for good ... So do not fear; I will provide for you and your little ones" (Genesis 50:20-21). What was Joseph doing? He was refusing to hold on to his brothers' offense, entrusting himself to him who judges justly, just as the Lord Jesus himself did (1 Peter 2:23). Joseph didn't pretend that his brothers' betrayal didn't hurt or that their actions weren't evil. He acknowledged both—but because he entrusted everything to the Lord, Joseph was free. Through his forgiveness and the freedom it brought, God rescued an entire nation from famine through him.

CONFLICT

Bitterness corrodes, and forgiveness is the only way to prevent it from corroding you. But that does not mean there will be no points of conflict as you keep walking forward.

Some people talk about "no-fault" divorce, but I've never heard of a conflict-free divorce. Normally I shy away from conflict, but after our separation I wanted to win every argument. I was determined to take back the control I'd lost. While it felt great to stick up for myself, digging in my heels and holding to my position, it didn't always go as well as you might think. I barely listened to what my ex-husband said because I was convinced he was just repeating the same selfish opinions. I, of course, had thoughtful and fair solutions to every problem.

I'm sure you'll be shocked to hear that we didn't make progress on important issues. So what I offer here is wisdom that I learned slowly, mainly through my own mistakes.

If you find you can't agree on anything with your ex, ask the Lord to help you be quick to listen, slow to speak and slow to become angry (James 1:19). You can't win every battle, so be willing to compromise on issues that aren't

critical to you. Ask God to give you a calm heart, a clear mind, and a gracious tone so you won't be drawn into pointless arguments or escalate an already tense situation. Listen carefully in the moment, not only to your ex-spouse but also to the Lord, before you respond.

At the same time, don't feel pressured to give in just to avoid an argument. Think through the reasoning behind what's important to you beforehand, evaluating the short- and long-term implications. Run your ideas past trusted friends and listen to their advice as you brainstorm potential pitfalls and questions. Talk through what you value, distinguish between major issues and minor points, and then stand up for what's important to you.

If you're getting steamrolled or being gaslighted, or if situations are becoming increasingly intense, consider involving a third party such as a counselor or mediator. They can help keep the conversation civil and on point, which will make it easier to reach agreement. In those meetings, voice your opinions when you're tempted to hold back and don't cave just because the tension is uncomfortable.

I found that email is often the best way to keep the conversation from getting heated or derailed. For important or controversial topics, it is wise to write out what you want to say and ask a trusted friend to read it and offer suggestions. I have a recently divorced friend who started a text thread with a group of several people. She reached out to us for advice and ran by us her thoughts on important issues, potential texts, or emails. Someone was always able to respond quickly. If you're not comfortable doing that with others, perhaps wait a day or two before sending any potentially volatile email, text, or voicemail, and then reread or listen again to what you are planning to send, imagining that

someone besides your ex-spouse might read or hear it as well. If they did, would you be embarrassed by your language or tone? That can help clarify what you want to communicate without being inflammatory.

Sometimes you may feel unprepared for conflict, perhaps because your spouse has the edge over you in terms of power, verbal sparring, or finances. On the other hand, you may be more verbally skilled, and feel justified in blame-shifting, exaggerating, or being untruthful because you feel powerless. Don't believe the lie that you're in this all alone and that you need to resort to tactics that may be underhanded. When you feel overwhelmed, cry out to God: "Lord, I don't know what to do, but my eyes are on you. Please fight this battle for me!" (see 2 Chronicles 20:12, 17). God will defend you, and he will fight your battle with you and for you. And he will conquer all our enemies. After all, your true enemy is not your ex-spouse, though it might feel like it. No, your worst enemy is Satan, who wants to kill, steal, and destroy you, tempting you to be bitter, cruel, and deceitful. Don't let Satan deceive you.

BOUNDARIES

As Christians we're taught to turn the other cheek, giving up our rights rather than holding on to them. Yet Scripture also holds up the importance of boundaries. In many ways, spouses who've been abandoned are like widows, and Scripture says that the Lord "maintains the widow's boundaries" (Proverbs 15:25). Way back in Eden, God told Adam and Eve what was in and out of bounds for them, and explained the consequences of any disobedience in transgressing those boundaries—and he enforced them. God allowed people to draw boundaries around their land allotments—lines that needed to be respected (see

Deuteronomy 19:14). Boundaries apply to property and to relationships. They are areas we control, that are rightfully ours, that we must clearly delineate and maintain.

I'd never maintained strong boundaries prior to my divorce, so this didn't come naturally for me. But after my separation I realized I needed both to draw clear lines and to stick to them. I had to take care that I was not doing so to be vindictive or vengeful, but I did need to do it to protect myself and ensure I was being fairly treated. We don't set boundaries to change our ex-spouse; we set them so we can heal.

The first limit I set was met with outrage. My ex informed me that I'd sabotaged any future possibility of reconciliation. Instinctively, I wanted to go back on my decision, but my counselor and close friends were all adamant that I should stick to my boundaries. Everyone felt they were fair. The situation with my ex stayed tense, as I anticipated it would—but as I held to the boundary I had set, rather than feeling anxiety, I felt relief. I began going into interactions more calmly, unafraid that I'd give in and later regret it. Setting boundaries kept me from responding in anger, enabling me to maintain self-control. And my ex-husband began respecting my boundaries when I stated them and followed through on what I had said.

Your boundaries will be different from mine, but one common area to set limits on is communication. Don't feel pressured to respond when it's most convenient for your ex if it is inconvenient for you. If your ex-spouse is belittling you, yelling at you, or otherwise being verbally inappropriate, in person or over the phone, be clear that you won't tolerate that behavior. If you're comfortable, say you will take a ten-minute break, or set a timer to limit the discussion, or even continue it on another day. If they won't respect your wishes, you may need to limit your

communication to email. That way, both of you can calmly and respectfully think through what you want to say.

Physical and personal space boundaries are important, especially after a divorce. It's important that you feel safe where you live. You have the right to make sure your ex does not enter your home without permission, to expect them to text before they come, and to keep your interactions brief. If they violate that boundary, you could consider meeting (even to drop off your children) at a neutral location. Don't ever tolerate physical abuse—get yourself and your children to a safe place, call your friends for help, and report what happened to the police.

If you've let your ex trample your boundaries in the past, they may become indignant if you now start setting limits. Don't let their fury change your response. Simply reiterate what you've decided. You don't have to be unjust or unkind; you can be gracious but firm, letting your yes be yes and your no be no. Your ex may accuse you of being unreasonable, unyielding, or even unchristian, but don't let them manipulate you. At the same time, if you're unsure whether your position is reasonable, ask trusted friends for their advice.

AFTER THE BITTERNESS

It's hard to immediately be "for" someone who has hurt you so deeply. It's hard to pray that they'll flourish in their new life. And it's hard to want them to overcome a sin or struggle that led to your divorce, whether it be addiction or infidelity or abuse or abandonment. Many of us, if we're honest, don't really want our ex to become post-divorce the person we thought we married in the first place, only for that person to be a blessing and joy to someone who isn't us. So simply ask God to direct your prayers and to give you the attitude towards your ex that the Lord wants you to have. Ask the

Lord to bring you to a point where you are able to pray for them. God doesn't ask us to muster up anything that he will not actually do in us and for us.

I started this chapter by mentioning that I'd been rereading my old journals. As I turned each page, I relived every difficult encounter, remembering every painful detail. The incredible part was that I'd forgotten most of them. I was once certain that I would always carry every hurtful word with me, but by God's grace they were no longer part of me. When I finally remembered what I had long forgotten, I realized that I had truly healed.

My ex-husband remarried and, years later, I did too. We are now friends. A few years ago at my older daughter's wedding reception, he came up to me and said, "I want you to know that your decision to forgive me changed my life. It changed my relationship with the girls. I can't thank you enough." I realized forgiveness hadn't just changed me. It had changed him. It had changed my family. It had set us all free.

CHAPTER 4

THE LIES WE BELIEVE AND THE GRACE THAT WE NEED

In the previous chapter, we discussed how to move beyond bitterness, not holding on to the wrongs that were done to us. But of course, we ourselves are not perfect. So how do we know what we are truly responsible for and what we're unfairly carrying? Some of us tend to blame ourselves for everything, constantly replaying what we could have done differently. Others of us instinctively excuse ourselves, shifting the blame elsewhere. And most of us swing between the two, unsure of what's truly ours to own.

After my divorce I questioned everything about myself, so when outsiders implied that I was even partly to blame for what happened, it hit a nerve. I still remember reading an article weeks after my ex had left that made me even more insecure, and that may or may not have inspired my purchase of a dartboard. The author said, "After talking with thousands of married couples, I have seldom found a

loving, submissive woman with a husband who is abusive or immoral." He went on to encourage women to suffer with a quiet and patient spirit under any type of mistreatment. The article used Scripture to defend this position, sending me into a rage and solidifying my fear that most Christians were silently judging me for being divorced.

Please know I am not against submission. But biblical submission doesn't mean putting up with abuse, and a lack of submission cannot be the underlying cause of a spouse's abusive or immoral behavior. My ex felt that I modeled biblical submission and encouraged me to give talks on it, which I did. But my submission did not save my marriage.

At the same time, I wasn't blameless in my marriage. Far from it. I acted self-righteously, believing I was never wrong. I said unkind things with a condescending tone. I was critical when I could have been compassionate. And that's just for starters.

That's the tension—discerning what is and isn't actually ours to own. I had to learn to separate what was truly my responsibility from what others tried to put on me. Maybe you've wrestled with that too. Perhaps you've been unfairly blamed for things outside of your control, or maybe there are places where God is gently convicting you. We all need wisdom to see the difference.

SEPARATING TRUTH FROM LIES

Divorce made me doubt myself, whispering lies that I was all too willing to believe. Here are some of the lies I told myself and the truths I needed to hear.

LIE: I WASN'T ENOUGH, OR MAYBE I WAS TOO MUCH

I thought something was inherently wrong with me. Do you wonder whether your spouse would have kept

their promises if you were more attractive, in better shape, smarter, more athletic, funnier, less needy, not so talkative, or more outgoing?

TRUTH: I AM ENOUGH AS I AM

My worth is not defined by my ex's actions. We are all defined by God's love for us. You are made in God's image and are inherently valuable, deserving of love and respect, and God wants you to know that. Don't let your spouse's words or actions devalue you.

LIE: IF I'D ACTED DIFFERENTLY, THIS WOULDN'T HAVE HAPPENED

I assumed it was somehow my fault. Perhaps you're beating yourself up, wondering whether, if you'd been more attentive, supportive or fun, or had taken on different responsibilities, this wouldn't have happened.

TRUTH: YOU'RE NOT RESPONSIBLE FOR SOMEONE ELSE'S ACTIONS

I wasn't responsible for the choices my ex made. Everyone is accountable for their own actions, so don't blame yourself or feel guilty about a situation you couldn't control.

LIE: I FAILED TO NOTICE THE WARNING SIGNS OR TO FIX THE RELATIONSHIP

I felt responsible for fixing our relationship. Perhaps you're wondering whether you could have saved your marriage if you had noticed signs of trouble earlier and had initiated something—conversations, changes, counseling, or some other kind of intervention.

TRUTH: YOU CANNOT SAVE A RELATIONSHIP BY YOURSELF

Since marriage involves two people, I couldn't put the burden solely on myself to figure out what was wrong. Each person needs to be honest about what's going on with them. You might reflect on when your situation changed in order to learn from that, but don't take responsibility for what isn't yours to own.

Just identifying the lies and reading the truth won't automatically change your perception. But it is a first step. Whenever you realize you are putting yourself down and accepting responsibility for what was never your fault, begin replacing it with the truth. Keep reminding yourself that you are a beloved child of God and ask him to keep putting what's true in front of you.

WHERE HEALING BEGINS

I want you to heal from the pain you've endured. For me, an integral part of healing was looking at my own heart and seeing areas where I needed to change. We've all been wounded, and we've all wounded others. None of us are completely innocent.

If you're like me, those words might make you feel defensive. Perhaps your ex deeply wronged you, but now somehow you're the one under a microscope, with strangers and friends speculating on what you're doing wrong. Please know that this chapter is not meant to elicit guilt or condemnation but rather to move you toward wholeness. Our sin entangles us—recognizing what's holding us back will help us to grow and to heal.

Let's begin by praying:

Search me, O God, and know my heart; test me and know my anxious thoughts. Point out anything in

> *me that offends you and lead me along the path of everlasting life. (Psalm 139:23-24, NLT)*

Then, as you ask God to search your heart, you'll likely become aware of ways in which you've been tempted to turn your back on God and find relief on your own. Satan wants to exploit your pain, pushing you into anger and bitterness or swamping you with guilt. He wants to pull you away from God when you need him most. In the Garden of Gethsemane, Jesus told his disciples to pray that they wouldn't fall into temptation (Luke 22:39). He knew that in the coming hours, days, and perhaps even years of suffering, each would have unique temptations that they needed to bring to God.

While everyone's struggles are particular to their temperament and past experiences, I'm going to group these struggles into three areas: the destructive ways in which we respond to ourselves, to others, and to God. Each destructive path will promise relief from the pain, but none will ever deliver.

RESPONDING TO OURSELVES

It takes time and work to process what you've been through, but most of us want to feel better immediately. It's much easier to find instant relief by numbing yourself from feeling pain, but that numbing will also keep you from feeling anything good like joy and hope.

If you have been looking for relief through illicit drugs, excessive alcohol, pornography, or gambling, I encourage you to get help for those habits or addictions (especially if they predated your divorce and perhaps contributed to it). It takes courage to admit your struggles and reach out for support.

Even if you don't wrestle with those more recognized

addictions, we all have unhealthy ways of coping. Take a moment to think about where you find comfort when you're upset. Everything on the list below offers a momentary escape, but instead of fixing your problems, each of them can end up adding to them.

- *Alcohol.* It may have started as enjoying a glass of wine or a cocktail with friends, but maybe it's moved to drinking several glasses or a bottle by yourself to unwind.
- *Food.* Our bodies need nutrition, and you may find delight in eating good food. But maybe now it's moved to overeating and binging on junk food to numb your pain.
- *Entertainment.* TV, movies, beach reads, video games, and social media can all be fun ways to temporarily disengage from what's happening around you. But maybe you're getting lost in a fantasy world, increasingly disconnected from the real one. Maybe it's what you turn to when reality feels too hard.
- *Activity.* Working, hobbies, fitness, and outside activities are all important parts of life. But maybe now you're immersing yourself in one area, pushing aside everything else, ignoring the signs that it's controlling you.
- *Relationships.* We are made for connection and relationships. But maybe now you're looking for love and acceptance through premature relationships and physical involvement to fill your emptiness.

My own overarching struggle is overworking and looking for my worth in productivity. I feel driven to be busy, and

I want everything I do to produce something visible. And when I'm not working, I struggle with coping mechanisms like shopping, eating chocolate, and wanting approval—each, for me, offers a momentary rush of adrenaline.

I can easily justify buying things under the pretense of shopping for what I "need"—a set of pens for writing, the perfect lamp, or yet another crisp white-collared shirt on clearance. (For the record, I own at least five. Striped ones don't count.) And while I might laugh about my love for dark chocolate—something I've faithfully eaten every night for 30 years—it's worth pausing to ask why I feel the urge to treat myself so often.

We all have go-to comforts—things that promise a quick hit of satisfaction. But are they filling a deeper need that only God can really satisfy? Temporary rewards often just leave us waiting for the next thing to distract us, but they don't give us peace. What small habits or indulgences do you turn to for comfort? And what would it look like to bring those longings to God instead?

RESPONDING TO OTHERS

Divorce impacts all our relationships. I found that I lashed out at some people—primarily those with whom I felt safest. I pulled away from several friends and expected too much from others. And I still wanted to please everyone. I'm going to list the typical ways in which people struggle in their relationships. If you can't identify with any of them, don't worry. Just ask your children or friends if they see any of these tendencies in you. (Mine were happy to oblige.)

ANGER

It's natural to be angry after a divorce if you've been wounded. You may scream, become combative, or throw things. Or you may be passive-aggressive by being

sarcastic or rude, coldly plotting revenge, or subtly humiliating others. The target could be your children, people you envy, those who have not supported you, or your ex. My anger felt uncontrollable at times—I remember pouring out words that felt really good in the moment but that I later regretted.

I've learned that responding to someone else's anger with a soft answer often de-escalates the situation. What immediately jumps to my mind in conflict is a hostile tone or biting sarcasm—blaming others to deflect attention from myself. But when I have the presence of mind to say, "Help me understand why you're responding this way," I've been amazed at how it defuses the situation.

Not all anger is wrong. When you consider the injustice of your situation, or other people's mistreatment, it's appropriate to be angry. The Bible doesn't tell us never to be angry, but it does caution us about how easily anger can lead to sin: "Be angry and do not sin; do not let the sun go down on your anger" (Ephesians 4:26). The key is letting anger move you to fight against injustice while still holding on to self-control and patience.

PULLING AWAY OR PUSHING TOWARDS OTHERS

We were created to live in healthy, life-giving community; but under stress we may pull away from others or aggressively push towards them. Both of those are broken responses. If we feel shamed by what happened, we may grow determined not to trust again and therefore find it easier to isolate ourselves than risk rejection and misunderstanding. After my ex left, I hated being in big groups and even dropped out of my church small group because I felt uncomfortable, wondering what people thought. It takes courage to trust others, letting them into our lives.

At other times, we may be determined that others must

meet our needs, no matter what. You may be preoccupied with your issues and forget there's a lot happening in your friends' lives, assuming they should always be available for you. I did just that with one of my closest friends—all I expected her to do was drop everything and listen to me, regardless of what she was doing. I couldn't figure out why she kept acting as if her family was a priority. I mean, what could possibly have been more important than my problems? I slowly learned that only God could carry all my burdens.

TRYING TO PLEASE EVERYONE

While it's natural to want others to like you, it's unhealthy to be consumed with wanting approval, avoiding conflict, and saying yes even when you don't want to. People-pleasers are afraid of the consequences if they set boundaries, giving others power that only God should have. I do that. It looks like a godly choice to outsiders, but I'm really looking for people to validate me.

This struggle to please was even more evident after my separation when I wrote this in my journal:

> *"I wanted to be loved and admired without condemnation or criticism, and so all my actions reflected that. Different people thought I should do different things, so sometimes I felt caught in the crossfire, wondering who was more important to please. It wasn't out of righteousness—it was out of my sinful desires. It looked like righteousness. People thought I was a saint. And I thought so too. And I resented any comments otherwise. Didn't people know how much I'd put up with?"*

It's hard to bear the emotional pain after divorce, so we try to shift our pain to others in subtle and overt ways—through anger, isolation, dependence, or wanting

approval. We're often blind to what we're doing, so we need God to open our eyes.

RESPONDING TO GOD

Though only God can truly hold your pain, you may hesitate to go to him. Perhaps, since God hasn't answered your faithful prayers—both before and after the divorce—you're wondering what the point of faithfulness is, especially when people who disregard God seem to be prospering. The psalmist Asaph confessed:

> *As for me, I almost lost my footing. My feet were slipping, and I was almost gone. For I envied the proud when I saw them prosper despite their wickedness ... Did I keep my heart pure for nothing? (Psalm 73:2-3, 13, NLT)*

Do you feel that your faithfulness was for nothing? Are you trying to understand why your ex seems to be flourishing while you're left floundering? I wrestled with that. It all seemed colossally unfair. Even non-Christians who cared nothing about God seemed to have incredible marriages and families. It was hard not to be jealous of them. Yet, like Asaph, I realized things are never as they seem. In the midst of his questioning, Asaph turned and declared:

> *Yet I still belong to you; you hold my right hand. You guide me with your counsel, leading me to a glorious destiny. Whom have I in heaven but you? I desire you more than anything on earth. My health may fail, and my spirit may grow weak, but God remains the strength of my heart; he is mine forever. (v 23-26, NLT)*

God has purposes and plans that we don't understand, but by faith we can believe that they are for our best. We may not see how what's happened to us could possibly be good, but we can trust that God hasn't made a mistake. One day,

we may understand more. But in the meantime, God is holding your hand, guiding you with his counsel, and will bring you into glory. He will never leave you. All you need to do is cling to him.

But right now, in your pain, the promise of God's presence may not feel particularly meaningful to you. Maybe divorce has shaken your faith, and you feel abandoned by God or furious at him for not honoring your tireless efforts to make your marriage work. Satan wants you to believe that God has let you down so that you'll resist opening the Bible and you'll stop praying. And the more distant God feels, the less you'll want to engage with him.

When you're deceived by someone who's supposed to love you, it can be hard to believe and trust God's love. I get it. And when you don't trust the love of God, it's easier to deal with your pain by distracting yourself or getting angry rather than turning to God. Besides, maybe you're wondering how you can be sure of God's love.

So let me tell you a story. Or rather, let Jesus tell you a story.

A CLEAR ILLUSTRATION OF GOD'S LOVE: THE PRODIGAL SON PARABLE

There was once a father with two sons (see Luke 15:11-32). The younger demanded his inheritance early—a shocking request, essentially wishing his father dead. The father granted it, selling part of his estate to give his son the money. The son left, squandering everything on reckless living. When a famine hit, he ended up feeding pigs, starving and alone.

Desperate, he decided to return home—not as a son (it was too late for that, surely) but as a servant. He knew he had forfeited his place in the family, though he still trusted

in his father's goodness to accept him back as a worker. But he had underestimated his father. Before he even reached home, his father saw him from afar and ran to embrace him, throwing his arms around his son's neck without even a word of reproach. As the son began his apology, the father was already dressing him in the best robe and throwing a feast to celebrate. His lost son had come home.

But the other, older son refused to join the celebration. He had obeyed every rule and worked hard every day, and now he felt overlooked. "All these years I've slaved for you," he said to his father, "yet you never threw me a party." To which the father responded, "You are always with me, and everything I have is yours. But we had to celebrate and rejoice, because this brother of yours was dead and is alive again; he was lost and is found" (Luke 15:31-32, CSB).

THE FATHER'S EXTRAVAGANT LOVE

The father's love is unmistakable and immeasurable. Picture him running down the road to greet his younger son. That is a shocking act of self-humiliation for a man of his status. Picture him leaving his home to plead with his elder son to join the celebration. In both cases, he moves toward his children rather than waiting for them to come to him. This is the picture of God coming to us in Jesus. When all else feels broken or confusing, Jesus is the great declaration of God's love. Like this father, God is not distant or passive—he is actively seeking, welcoming, and restoring. Whether we are lost in rebellion or resentment, his love is constant, and his invitation is open.

The question in the story is... will the sons realize it?

For a while it seemed that the younger son would miss it. He thought freedom meant breaking away from his father's authority. He wanted the benefits of his father's wealth without the relationship. But when his reckless

and selfish choices left him empty and ashamed, he headed home; life apart from his father wasn't what he'd imagined. Even then, as we saw, he underestimated his father's love. He expected to earn a place as a servant—yet his father restored him as his son as soon as he returned.

Like this son, we often believe we must work our way back to God. But repentance is simply returning, trusting in God's mercy rather than our merit.

In the end, though, it was the older son who missed it. He had stayed home, obeyed the rules, and worked hard—but his heart was far from his father. He resented the love shown to his brother because he saw obedience as a transaction. He was certain that his faithfulness should have earned him something more. In the end, he was as lost as his younger brother had been.

How easily we can fall into the same trap—believing we deserve God's favor because of our goodness and resenting his grace when it's given freely to others. Perhaps the greatest danger for the older brother—and for us—is focusing on the younger brother's behavior and how undeserving he is, rather than our own need for grace. The older brother needed to repent—not of obvious rebellion, but of his self-righteousness and resentment.

COMING HOME

Both sons, then, needed to repent. The younger had to return home physically, but the older needed to return home in his heart. At the heart of repentance is choosing what we do with our sin: "We only have two options with sin: allow it to *turn us away* from the Father in shame or *turn us toward* the Father in surrender."[12]

Repentance is not about condemnation. There is no condemnation for those of us in Christ Jesus (Romans 8:1).

12 Julie Busler, *Hopeful Sorrow* (B&H Publishing Group, 2025), p. 152.

Repentance isn't about making someone feel like a worm, crippled by guilt. It's about realizing that our way isn't working and turning back to the Father's love. Repentance is choosing to come home. And the good news? The Father is already running toward you.

God's kindness leads us to repentance (Romans 2:4). He sees not just what we've done but what's been done to us. He understands the wounds we carry, the ways we've reacted, and the struggles we hide. Repentance is bringing those things to him—naming them, asking for forgiveness where we need to, and allowing him to cleanse us.

It reminds me of taking a shower. Whether we've been working in the dirt or just going about our day, we all get dirty. If we don't wash, we may not notice at first, but eventually the stench will be undeniable. Confession and repentance are like stepping into the water and letting it cleanse what we didn't even realize had built up.

The joy that follows is astounding. Repentance realigns us with God, freeing us from the weight of guilt and bitterness. It's the key to a growing, vibrant faith. As pastor Tim Keller put it, "The more we know we are forgiven, the more we repent; the faster we grow and change, the deeper our humility and joy."[13]

The most revered of Old Testament kings, David, gives us a famous model of repentance in Psalm 51. After his greatest failure, he didn't make excuses, but neither did he grovel in shame—he boldly asked God for a clean heart, a renewed spirit, and the joy of salvation. Why? Because he trusted in God's kindness.

And so can you.

---

13 Timothy Keller, *Prayer: Experiencing Awe and Intimacy with God* (Penguin Books, 2014), p. 211.

WHO ARE YOU?

I had known this parable for years, but it changed me when I read *The Prodigal God* by Tim Keller. These words pierced me—because I realized that I was the elder brother:

> *"Elder brothers expect their goodness to pay off, and if it doesn't, there is confusion and rage. If you think goodness and decency is the way to merit a good life from God, you will be eaten up with anger, since life never goes as we wish. You always feel that you are owed more than you are getting."*[14]

I realized that my anger at God wasn't just grief—it was entitlement. I thought my righteousness had earned me a good marriage. It was not about delighting in God; I'd been using God to get what I wanted.

So let me ask you, when it comes to your marriage, who are you in this parable?

Are you the younger son—the one who broke the covenant, disregarded your spouse, or ran after something else? Maybe you sought escape or excitement, only to realize it wasn't what you had hoped. And now you wonder if you even deserve a relationship with God.

Or are you the elder son—the faithful one who has done everything "right" yet feels overlooked or unfairly treated? Maybe you're tired of doing the right thing and feel resentful that God hasn't rewarded you. You expected life to go a certain way, and when it didn't, you felt cheated.

No matter who you are, the Father is waiting. All you have to do is turn toward home.

---

14 Timothy Keller, *The Prodigal God: Recovering the Heart of the Christian Faith* (Penguin Group, 2008), p. 52.

WHAT DO I NEED TO CARRY?

Some burdens are unfairly placed on us, meant to weigh us down with false guilt and shame. At other times, we truly need to repent, recognizing where we've fallen short, coming to God for forgiveness, and asking him to realign our hearts with his.

That can be tricky to navigate. Left to ourselves, we can be too harsh, blaming ourselves for things that aren't our fault, or too lenient, excusing what we need to own. That's why we need the wisdom of God's word and the perspective of trusted believers. We need friends who will help us lay down burdens we were never meant to carry and who love us enough to point out where we may be blind to our own faults.

Regardless of what we uncover, we do so in the presence of a Father who welcomes us in—who does not condemn us but restores us. So as you reflect on the details of your own situation and your own responses, ask yourself honestly:

Do I need to feel guilty for this?

If the answer is *no*, let it go. You've been listening to a lie.

If the answer is *yes*, bring it to God. He is ready to forgive.

Either way, your burden is not yours to carry alone. And no matter what, your Father is always waiting with open arms.

CHAPTER 5

REASSESSING, REBUILDING, AND REKINDLING JOY

After my divorce, I thought my life was ruined. My dreams were dead—how could I risk dreaming again? I once believed that hard work, sacrifice, and prayer would guarantee a good marriage. Now I couldn't be sure of anything. Hoping felt foolish, just inviting more disappointment.

During that painful season, God literally brought a dead bush back to life. It wasn't just any shrub—it was the camellia we'd planted in memory of our infant son Paul. When we moved, I'd lovingly replanted it by our new front door, but the summer heat was merciless. Its leaves dried up and fell off until only brittle twigs remained. The lawn guy eventually chopped it down, insisting it was an eyesore.

All winter long, I cringed at seeing the decaying stump where the camellia bush used to be. It was the same winter that my husband left. The empty space represented layers of loss—painful reminders of what had been but never

would be again. I usually looked away as I walked up the front steps; the dead shrub was an all-too-fitting picture of my life.

But one spring day, I noticed a tiny green shoot pushing through the dead wood. Within weeks, glossy leaves unfurled. Though the summer's heat had destroyed its branches, its roots had survived. After a brutal season of dormancy and pruning, it was regenerating. I moved the camellia to a cooler spot, and it flourished, eventually bursting into stunning white blooms—more beautiful than ever before.

Seeing that camellia gave me hope. If God could revive that seemingly dead plant, maybe he could do the same for me, since he "gives life to the dead and calls into existence the things that do not exist" (Romans 4:17b). Maybe one day, I would thrive again too.

Perhaps you're wondering if your life will ever be beautiful after all you've lost. Maybe you see nothing but wasted years. Maybe you're still in winter, and everything around you looks lifeless. If that's where you are, know that your story is not over yet. God may be about to spring into blossom what currently looks barren. It all begins with rebuilding.

REBUILDING

The hardest part of rebuilding for me was recognizing that the old structure was gone. There was nothing to go back to. I'd begged God to change my husband's heart for so long that I couldn't imagine any other outcome that seemed good. I'd put my life on pause, convinced that I'd soon return to the life I'd built. Yet as my ex became increasingly committed to staying where he was, I asked the Lord what I needed to see differently. One morning, as I read Jeremiah 29, I noticed that God told his people

in exile to settle down and build where they were—to seek the welfare of the city they were in rather than just waiting to return. I sensed that that passage was God's invitation to stop clinging to the past and to step into the future.

That perspective shift was disorienting and exhilarating. For the first time, I felt the freedom to make new plans—a freedom that brought both hope and fear.

How would I rebuild? I thought of the Israelites, once they had finally returned to their land, rebuilding the temple after its destruction. Their progress was slow and discouraging. They faced constant setbacks, mixed emotions, and opposition. Yet as they worked, God encouraged them to remember, "Not by might, not by power, but by my Spirit, says the LORD" (Zechariah 4:6). I memorized those words and would repeat them throughout the day, reminding myself that it wasn't about my strength or skill—it was about God's power working through me.

Rebuilding is slow work—day by day, brick by brick. Progress can feel invisible. God encouraged the Israelites not to despise small beginnings, promising they would one day rejoice when the work was complete (v 10). I clung to that truth, learning to celebrate even the smallest victories, trusting they would lead to something greater.

You might feel stuck at the beginning of your own rebuilding, eager for everything to be settled, anxious about the process. This is a normal part of growth and change. It may not be at the pace that you want, but be assured that God is at work, even in the long delays.

To rebuild, we need a vision for the future. What would you want your life to look like in a few years? Don't let past disappointments crush your new dreams. Don't let your fears, insecurities, and self-doubts keep you from imagining a life more beautiful than you thought possible.

You get to write this next chapter and build something new with the Lord. Let's begin by exploring where you are now and where you could be.

FIGURING OUT WHERE YOU ARE

As I encourage you to envision your future, I want to be honest: when I started, I had no idea what I wanted my future to look like. I had no goals or vision beyond getting out of bed and making it through the day. If you feel the same way, I hope this chapter helps you take the first step.

Months after my ex left, my sister Shalini flew down because she knew I needed help. She wanted me to start living intentionally, not just survive. We camped out at Panera Bread for hours, fueled by mediocre coffee and egg soufflés, while a friend watched my daughters.

Together, we evaluated my life piece by piece: what was working, what wasn't, what felt draining, and what brought joy. I couldn't get rid of everything that was draining (for instance, I had to keep my kids), but there were some things I could cut out immediately. We mapped out my daily routines, responsibilities, weekends, finances, and how I spent my time. It felt overwhelming to tackle these alone, but with my sister guiding the conversation I could finally see things clearly.

If you're a verbal processor like me, invite a trusted friend to talk through things; or, if you prefer, do it by yourself. Start by reflecting on these six key areas: Faith, Fun, Fitness (emotional and physical), Finances, Family, and Friendships. For each category, ask yourself...

1. What's working?

2. What's not working?

3. What would I like this area to eventually look like?

Before we dive into the first four categories (we'll handle the last two in subsequent chapters), I want to help you re-envision what you already have.

REFRAMING AND REARRANGING

I found that reframing my situation—seeing it with fresh eyes and looking for the positives—shifted my perspective. A few months before my ex left, we'd picked out a wall stencil together that quoted Joshua 24:15: "As for me and my house, we will serve the LORD" After it went up on the wall above our front door, he hated it. I considered painting over it after he left—it felt like a painful reminder of what our family used to be.

But then I realized: those words still mattered. They were my vision for the new life I was building with God. Every time I passed it, the verse reminded me that this was a new home, a new beginning.

Reframing can change how you see your situation. Instead of being left, maybe it was God's rescue. Instead of downsizing, maybe it's a fresh start. Feeling overwhelmed could be an opportunity to experience God's provision in unexpected ways.

It took me months to take down old family photos that included my ex, because I didn't want to upset my daughters. But I knew moving forward meant removing constant reminders of the past. I boxed up those pictures, saving them for my girls if they ever wanted them.

The hardest place for me was our walk-in closet. My ex left most of his clothes behind and would occasionally stop by to grab something. When my sister Shalini visited, she was horrified to see his clothes still hanging there. "We're boxing these up now," she insisted, marching to the attic for cardboard boxes.

She started yanking clothes off hangers, stuffing them

into boxes with fierce determination. When I suggested folding them, she laughed and said, "He's lucky I'm not going to leave all these cardboard boxes outside in the rain." Her boldness made me laugh—and something shifted. I joined her, ripping clothes off hangers, boxing them up, and punching the contents down. It felt freeing.

But when we finished, the emptiness of the closet hit me. The vacant shelves, the bare hangers, the cobwebs—it mirrored the emptiness I felt inside.

What I didn't realize was that Shalini already had a vision for the space. She suggested turning it into a sanctuary. We moved a table under the rack where his suits once hung, added a chair, and hung a bulletin board above it. We decorated the shelves with scarves, pictures, framed verses and my favorite Willow Tree figurines. Then we placed my Bible and journal on the table.

That closet became the most beautiful place in my home—a quiet space where I met with God. What once had reminded me of loss became a symbol of his restoration. Every time I walked in, I was reminded that God can make all things new.

FAITH: LETTING GOD REBUILD YOU

The first area to evaluate is faith, which we've been considering all along in this book. My faith changed completely through my separation and divorce. I'd always had set-apart time with God, but sometimes it felt more like a task to check off than a gift to enjoy. But when I was desperate, with nowhere to turn but to God, it became the best part of my day. I wasn't just reading Scripture to learn more about God; I was lingering over it to meet him. The difference between reading and lingering is like the difference between reading about bread and tasting it fresh from the oven: warm, crusty, and melting with butter.

Somewhere in those encounters, I fell in love with Jesus. Falling in love releases endorphins that make us happy, which is how I felt when I sat down with my Bible. I felt seen, known, and treasured, and I realized that the Lord's presence was far more precious than the answers I had thought I needed.

Of course, not every day felt like that. Some mornings, opening my Bible still felt more like duty than delight. Maybe that's true for you too. Some days, you may struggle to focus, pray, or even want to show up. That's okay. God sees your heart, and he knows what you need. Sometimes, he may meet you in breathtaking ways. Other times, he will simply give you the grace to press on.

God has wired all of us differently, so don't compare your commitment, emotions, or knowledge with other people and assume you're falling short. Your relationship with the Lord is unique—it won't look like mine or anyone else's. What's important is showing up, even if it's just for a few minutes, trusting that he will meet you there. Start small. Get up a little earlier, read a psalm or part of a Gospel, and let your relationship with the Lord grow at its own pace.

One of my favorite morning prayers has become "Let me hear in the morning of your steadfast love, for in you I trust. Make me know the way I should go, for to you I lift up my soul" (Psalm 143:8). I didn't pray that verse back then, but it would have given me words when I didn't have any. It might be a helpful place for you to start from today.

For me back then, mornings often looked like pulling on my robe, sitting in my prayer closet, and asking God to help me. Some days, I arrived eager and expectant; other days, I showed up out of sheer habit, hoping he would meet me anyway. Often, I'd whisper, "My soul clings to the

dust; give me life according to your word" (Psalm 119:25). Then I'd wait expectantly and listen.

I wrote in my journal:

> *"I'm amazed at your provision. I come to this quiet time with anticipation—you have filled me beyond measure and met me in incredible ways every day. It's been nine months since [my ex] left, and it's unbelievable how tangible you feel."*

The more time I spent with God, the more I realized that I could ask him anything. He could do more than I could ask or imagine. Nothing was too hard for him (Jeremiah 32:17). I didn't need to see how it could happen; God could simply speak the word, and everything would change. These truths weren't just familiar Bible verses anymore—they became deeply personal promises.

My prayer life changed as well. For so long, I'd been oblivious to God's work in my life—a living proof of the truth that "God speaks time and again, but a person may not notice it" (Job 33:14, CSB). I began listening for God's voice and looking around for ways in which he was answering my prayers. The results were astonishing.

God can meet you as he met me. He doesn't simply love you—he's passionate about you. He sings songs over you. He longs to be with you.

FUN: FINDING WHAT MAKES YOU SMILE AGAIN

Fun was the last thing on my mind after my divorce, but I realized I needed to rediscover it in order to move forward. At first, I had no idea what would bring me joy. I felt disconnected from myself, unsure of what I liked or even of who I was. But divorce gave me a unique opportunity to rediscover myself.

So we got a dog.

"Fun" isn't the first word I'd use to describe that experience—puppy training felt like living with a 15-pound dictator who was determined to pull the stuffing out of every pillow he saw. My daughters promised to handle everything, and... well, you can guess how that went. I once went away for a weekend, and the girls didn't know they were expected to feed the dog, though they did wonder why he kept begging for food. Yet despite the chaos that accompanied him, little Mocha also brought joy into our home. He made sure all of us felt unconditionally loved and wanted.

Another way I figured out "fun" was going to a coffee shop and brainstorming things that made me feel alive. At first, I could barely think of anything—I'd felt lost for so long. But as I kept writing, memories surfaced: coffee with friends, doing anything artistic, laughing till my sides hurt.

I began experimenting—trying new things and rediscovering old loves. I created playlists and listened to them on repeat. I picked up watercolor pencils and doodled in a notebook. I intentionally sought out humor because I needed to laugh. My daughters and I discovered a new comedian—quoting his best lines became our unofficial family language. We created new traditions, watched TV together, and discovered new places to eat.

Since I was homeschooling my daughters when my ex left, I had no time to myself. So a friend suggested I go on a silent retreat. She thought would be refreshing; I thought it sounded like torture. But I took her advice, which was a huge step for this extrovert verbal-processor, and I'm so thankful I did. At first I felt fidgety, unsure of what to do. But after a while, I saw the beauty of solitude and silence. I came home restored and renewed, with a calmness, clarity and closeness to God that kept me regularly going back for years.

After asking God for direction on what to do next, several friends in the same week encouraged me to start writing. My writing experience had been limited to personal journaling and some questionable attempts at humorous Christmas letters, so I enrolled in a memoir-writing class at a local college. After a few weeks, I was hooked. My classmates consistently described my writing as "plain," which I optimistically interpreted as "clear and timeless." Somehow, even after such a dubious start, I eventually became a writer. Discovering what brought me joy changed my life.

Everyone has different things that make them happy. In writing this book, I asked friends who'd gone through divorce what they did to find joy. Here's what they shared:

- One started walking daily—not for exercise but just to be outside and notice beauty.
- Another friend got her "colors" done—figuring out which colors were most flattering on her—and refreshed her wardrobe.
- Someone took up dancing, both around the house alone and out with friends.
- Several mentioned eating more healthily and therefore feeling healthier.
- Several guys started exercising, with many going to the gym more regularly. One recommitted to Bible study, and another planned get-togethers with friends rather than watching TV.
- One woman booked monthly massages; others began attending plays, watching the sunrise, or reading good books.

- One mom committed to laughing as much as possible—hosting game nights, doing silly TikTok dances with her kids, and looking for funny Instagram memes and videos.

Do any of these resonate with you? Moving forward means rediscovering yourself—or perhaps getting to know yourself for the first time. Maybe you haven't felt excited about anything in a long time, but I invite you to pause and consider:

- What brings you joy, or what brought you joy in a past season?
- What makes you feel alive?
- Is there something that you've always wanted to try?

You don't need to dive into anything daring. Start where you are. Rearrange your furniture, hang new artwork, or decorate your space exactly how you want. You don't have to spend much—thrift stores and DIY projects can create something fresh and distinctively you.

God has beautiful plans for your future. Believe that he's creating something good—even now.

FITNESS: PHYSICAL AND EMOTIONAL WELL-BEING

After my separation, with so much to manage and facing constant change, I focused on what felt urgent—and that didn't include self-care. I cringed when I looked in the mirror—if I bothered looking at all. The truth was that I felt unattractive, which made me care less about my appearance. What was the point of caring at all?

Do you see your beauty? Do you notice your strengths, or do you fixate on what you don't like? When was

the last time you truly looked in the mirror, not with judgment but with kindness?

RECLAIMING EMOTIONAL HEALTH

I spent months in my counselor's office, unraveling the pain and lies I'd carried for years. The self-doubt. The shame. The belief that I wasn't enough. Therapy helped me unpack what had happened, what I needed to accept, and what I needed to change.

At first, I cried through nearly every session, rehashing hurtful things my ex had said and done. But slowly, my counselor helped me depersonalize what wasn't truly about me. Over time, my emotions stabilized, and my perspective shifted. I started seeing myself with more respect and confidence.

While counseling was invaluable for me, if you don't have the resources to access it, please don't feel that it's vital for healing. My friends were great to process things with, so consider asking a friend to sit down with you regularly and help you talk things through as well as pray with you. You might also think about asking Christian friends who have been through divorce about what podcasts, sermons, and books have helped them. Journaling is also a great form of therapy. Writing helped me process my thoughts, remember important events, and notice God's faithfulness. Looking back, I can see how much I grew and how clearly God answered my prayers through that difficult season.

RESTORING PHYSICAL HEALTH

After my separation, I was constantly exhausted. I wasn't sleeping, eating well, or exercising. I felt overwhelmed, foggy, and irritable—even more than normal, that is. I thought I didn't have time to take care of myself. The truth was, I couldn't afford not to.

As I saw myself burning out, I wrote in my journal, "I can't keep putting off things that will make me healthier. Like in an airplane, you have to put on your own mask first before helping others." Yes, my daughters needed me—but they needed a healthy me.

I knew sleep was important, though my teenagers always seemed to need deep, soul-searching conversations just when I was ready to collapse into bed. Even when I got into bed on time, worry often kept me awake. For the first time, I had to surrender my sleepless nights to God, asking him to calm my anxious heart.

Eating well, drinking water, and avoiding junk food can fuel your body and clear your mind. Exercise doesn't have to be extreme—don't rush out to join a gym or set unrealistic goals. Start small. Try a short daily walk—even just ten minutes. Walk alone and pray or invite a friend to join you. Balance is key. You matter. Taking care of yourself is essential—not just for you but for the people who love you. Healing begins when you recognize that you're worth the effort.

FINANCES AND MORE: TACKLING WHAT'S AHEAD

Finances terrified me. My ex had always handled them—I didn't even know how to log in to online banking. After swallowing my pride, I asked a friend to teach me the basics and then took a class on money management. Budgeting felt overwhelming at first, but learning how to manage my finances boosted my confidence and gave me a sense of control. Just taking that first step made similar tasks feel less intimidating.

In addition to handling the money, my ex used to handle household tasks like fixing whatever broke, dealing with tech issues, and taking out the trash. We would always joke

that his "repair process" involved making things worse before calling a professional. Now I was able to skip the middleman. Particularly because of my physical disability, I knew I wouldn't be able to do everything myself. So I reached out to people from my church, and they took care of so many things for me—but I first had to ask.

If figuring out your finances feels impossible to you, start by asking God for help. Don't hope it will magically "work out" without your putting in any effort. If you can, find someone you trust, like a friend or church member, to walk you through the basics: income, expenses, savings, insurance, and debt. You may be surprised at how manageable it feels once you begin.

What else needs to be done in your life? What can you handle, and what requires help? Who could you ask? Just like budgeting money, you have to budget your time and energy too.

Feeling overwhelmed is normal. Elisabeth Elliot's words, "Do the next thing," became my go-to phrase.[15] I didn't have to solve everything at once. I just needed to do the next thing, and so do you. Make a grocery list. Start a load of laundry. Ask someone for advice. You don't have to do it all at once. Just do the next thing.

GRATITUDE: FINDING JOY WHERE YOU ARE

After my divorce, there was so much I didn't like about my situation. Nothing felt stable or secure. The more I focused on what I lacked, the more discontented I became. So I started naming what I *did* have.

Each day, I wrote three things I was grateful for in my journal. Small things. Big things. Things I'd have missed

15 Justin Taylor, "Do the Next Thing," The Gospel Coalition, October 25, 2017; thegospelcoalition.org/blogs/justin-taylor/do-the-next-thing/ (accessed April 15, 2025).

if I hadn't paused to notice. Just having heat on a cold winter morning. A friend's kind text. An unexpected answer to prayer. A sense of God's presence.

I realized God had been with me all along—but I only noticed when I paid attention. I learned that being watchful for what God was doing led to being more thankful and prayerful (Colossians 4:2). He was constantly offering signs of his love.

I once felt my divorce had taken so much from me—hopes and dreams and years that I could never get back. But ultimately God gave me back much more than I lost. I learned I was strong. Resilient. Capable. Worthwhile. I discovered I could learn new things. I could dare to dream big. I could trust God with my life.

You may not see it yet, but through your pain God is inviting you into a deeper relationship with him. I wanted God to restore my marriage, but instead he restored me. He healed me, helped me love my life again, and filled me with hope for the future.

I'm praying he'll do the same for you. Don't fix your eyes on what's broken or missing. Live in hope, trust that God is already working, and believe this: he is writing a good story with your life.

CHAPTER 6

PARENTING ON EMPTY

"I hate you. No wonder dad left you!"

My daughter ran out into the night, slamming the door behind her. The glass on the door rattled, and I thought it would break, but not nearly as much as I was breaking inside.

"How did we come to this?" I wondered. It was after midnight. Though I didn't want to re-engage, I couldn't let an adolescent girl wander alone that late. I called a neighbor, and after an hour we finally spotted her curled up on the back porch. I persuaded her to come in, and she crawled into bed, while I lay awake for hours, wondering how I would ever get through this.

Parenting through my divorce was one of the hardest challenges I've ever faced. I have friends who had an amazing rapport with their children after their spouses left. Their families pulled together, grew closer than ever, and made beautiful new memories.

Those stories make me want to flip a table.

Our experience was the opposite—divorce pulled us apart. No one was enjoying family time together, least of all me.

My experience was one of parenting two adolescent daughters; yours is likely different. Maybe your children are younger or older. Maybe they don't live with you, and if that's the case, I imagine this chapter may be even harder to read. While single parenting was incredibly difficult, I was fortunate to have my daughters with me. If your children live primarily with your ex, or if you're navigating long-distance parenting, that loss of daily connection can bring a different kind of grief. Still, the underlying parenting principles hold true, no matter your situation.

Writing this chapter, I cringed at all the things I wish I'd done differently. You may already feel that way. Yet our failures point to how much we need Jesus. When we make mistakes, we can ask our kids for forgiveness. It's possible to repair and restore. It's not about never failing—it's about how we respond when we do.

MY WORLD AFTER DIVORCE: WORRIES

When my ex left, one of my primary concerns was of course for our children. We'd built a home filled with love and trust that was largely sheltered from the struggles other families faced. Overnight, that shelter was gone. Suddenly our children were navigating life as part of a broken family.

I worried about everything—their emotional well-being, future relationships, and faith. Would they pull away from friends? Struggle to fit in? Lose trust in marriage or men? How much should I tell them, and how would they process it all? My head spins remembering the weight of it all.

I'd always been careful—maybe even overprotective—about the shows they watched and the friends they spent time with. Now I couldn't shake the thought that we'd become *that* family—the one other protective parents whispered about and quietly steered their kids away from.

STRUGGLES

As a single parent I second-guessed every decision I made, especially when my daughters pushed back. I couldn't measure up to what two parents could provide, though I tried, and I constantly felt pulled in a hundred directions. Every meal, every school drop-off, every doctor's appointment was my responsibility. I was the one calling the repairman when something broke, getting up at 3 a.m. when someone was sick, talking past midnight about struggles at school, and helping with last-minute homework.

I went to every practice, every game, and every piano recital. (The latter was an indisputable act of love and sacrifice. If you've ever endured a piano recital that felt about 23 hours long, followed by the obligatory stale cookies and syrupy lemonade, you know exactly what I mean.) Yet, despite all I managed to do, I constantly felt I was failing. I focused on what I had missed, what I hadn't done, what I could have done better.

FAILURES

My daughters were crushed when their dad left. Since they struggled to put their feelings into words, their pain came out through their behavior instead. One daughter was reportedly bullying other kids, prompting calls from two concerned mothers who said she had publicly humiliated their children. Another night, a youth pastor from a nearby church called to tell me that my daughter had mentioned suicide to several people. One daughter would explode in anger and swear at me—at home, in store, and even in church. The more things spiraled out of control, the more I felt like the target for their frustration. I wasn't just their mom anymore; I was the villain, the embarrassing adult who could do nothing right.

Of course, my kids thought that I was the problem. Apparently, I chewed like a wildebeest, spoke too loudly in public, and was embarrassingly chatty to restaurant servers. Before their friends came over, I'd get clear instructions: "Can you not ask my friends questions? You're a little too eager to talk. Actually, could you just wait in your room till they leave?" (To be fair, to this day I still get similar comments before I meet their friends, so maybe it wasn't just the divorce.)

While I can laugh now at my children's comments, there wasn't much laughter back then. I exploded. I handed out escalating consequences—taking away phones, limiting screens, grounding them. The punishments would far outweigh their offenses, but they knew I wasn't strong enough, physically or emotionally, to consistently follow through anyway. In response, I took out my frustrations on my girls, overreacting to the slightest thing. At my worst, I threw a full glass of ice water on one daughter in frustration. On the bright side, I reassured myself, at least it wasn't hot coffee—or soup. I screamed that I couldn't wait for them to leave home and go to college. After one particularly horrible argument, I drove away to cool off, even as my precious daughter stood at the door, sobbing as she begged me to stay. I wish I could take back those moments.

I was in survival mode most days but was too ashamed to admit my failures. I placed enormous pressure on my children to be perfectly behaved around others. I became fixated on appearances, focused on what I could see and, more importantly, what everyone else could see. And with that fixation, I failed to truly see my daughters.

MOMENTS OF GRACE

I couldn't find the right balance in parenting; I was either too lenient or too strict. When I was discouraged about my

failures, a friend gently reminded me, "I know you're not perfect, but you are the perfect parent for them." I realized that God would equip me with everything I needed. He had chosen me to parent these girls.

One breakthrough came through an art project. My daughter was struggling to replicate the famous Japanese print *The Great Wave off Kanagawa*. After several failed attempts and many tears, I helped her outline the main design, pointing out the importance of paying attention to the details. As we worked side by side, she quietly said, "You are my Hokusai. You're the person I learn from—the one I watch and want to imitate."

Years later, she gave me a framed print of *The Great Wave*. It hangs in the room where I have my quiet time, a daily reminder that even when I can't see it, God is working.

LEANING ON GOD

My greatest fear was that my children would walk away from God and never trust him again. For months on end, they prayed every night that their father would come back to us. After a year, I wondered how those prayers were impacting their faith. I knew that God could grant our requests, but I also knew that the answer might not be what we'd hoped.

During that time, I was memorizing different psalms, and one daughter asked me to recite what I was learning as I tucked her in each night. Once, when I got to Psalm 34:4—"I sought the LORD, and he answered me and delivered me from all my fears"—she asked, "Why hasn't God answered me? Why hasn't God brought Daddy back? Why hasn't he delivered me from my fears?"

I wasn't prepared for that question. At least not then. I wanted to rush in with a beautifully biblical and theological explanation, but I didn't have one. So, through tears, I told

her the truth—I didn't know why. I didn't understand why our prayers weren't being answered in the way we hoped. I was struggling too. I didn't want to dismiss her questions or pretend I had it all figured out.

Meanwhile, I saw their faith slowly unraveling. We had once had meaningful family devotions, but my efforts were later met with eye rolls and disinterest. One daughter, who had been baptized months before her father left, declared she didn't want anything to do with my God anymore. He was no longer *her* God—just mine.

As those dark days stretched into months and even years, I prayed like never before. Lamentations 2:19 says, "Arise, cry out in the night ... Pour out your heart like water before the presence of the Lord! Lift your hands to him for the lives of your children." Many nights, I did just that. I couldn't control their world, but I could cry out to God for mercy.

I begged God for wisdom (James 1:5), fully aware that I didn't know how to navigate the challenges ahead or what was best for my children. Without fail, God gave me insight exactly when I needed it. I prayed specific prayers for each daughter, inserting their names into specific verses. I recently found an old prayer card where I'd written...

> *"Lord, help _____ to trust in you with all her heart, and not depend on her own understanding. May she seek your will in all she does. Please direct her paths and show her which way to go as you have promised. Proverbs 3:5-6."*

I prayed daily that they both would turn back to the Lord, knowing God would have to do that work. While I kept teaching them Scripture, I realized that seeing *me* read my Bible had a greater impact than my constantly quoting Bible verses or turning situations into "life lessons." And I

realized that praying was the most powerful thing I could do. They each walked their own winding paths, but over time their faith became real. They wrestled with God and discovered his faithfulness for themselves. I'd so desperately wanted a picture-perfect story in which my daughters grew up in an intact family, but God had a different plan. A *better* plan. One that forged a deeper, more authentic faith than the "perfect" life I'd imagined for them.

If your children are not interested in faith right now, don't despair. Keep praying. Don't assume that this moment, or this year, is an indication of their whole future. It's okay for them to question. It might just lead to a stronger faith.

SHOWING UP WHILE STAYING STRONG

While I sometimes wished my children would empathize with me and make my life easier, that wasn't their role. My job was to be emotionally present for them, attuned to their feelings, and to provide a secure space where they could express their emotions like anger, sadness, and frustration. I was their safe place for them to pour out their emotions—but mistakenly I took it personally. They were processing their own pain, and I was sometimes caught in the crossfire.

A friend once shared that after her parents' divorce, her mother heavily leaned on her for emotional support—asking for advice, venting about her father, and even asking her to spy on him. At first, she felt valued, but it quickly became overwhelming. She couldn't process her own grief because she was too busy managing her mom's. Her story showed me that I couldn't ask my daughters to carry my emotions or act as my confidantes. That was a role they were never meant to fill. Instead, I needed to lean on friends and family for support.

In my effort not to overwhelm them, I probably went too far in the other direction. I rarely let them see me cry, pretending to be strong while grieving privately. Later, they told me they wished I'd been more open—not to carry my burdens but because seeing me process my emotions might have helped them process their own.

If your children are taking their emotions out on you, remember that it's likely not personal. They are dealing with their own hurt, and you may be the easiest target for their frustration. If they ask you, be willing to honestly share some of your struggles with them. But even with adult children, remember that they are not your emotional caretakers. They have their own pain to process, and oversharing can place unnecessary pressure on them.

NURTURING YOUR CHILDREN

As parents, we are called to nurture our children, not exasperate them (Ephesians 6:4). I frequently frustrated my children by focusing on what they were doing wrong rather than encouraging them. I wish I had been more "quick to hear, slow to speak, [and] slow to anger" (James 1:19).

QUICK TO LISTEN

One of my regrets is not paying closer attention to what was happening in my children's worlds. I asked them questions but didn't try to understand what was behind their words. When I'd ask one daughter how lunch was, she'd shrug and say something like, "Okay, I guess. Stop asking questions." What I didn't know was that she ate lunch in the bathroom stall every day.

I forgot how much my kids' worlds had been turned upside down. They too were trying to find their way—to figure out who they were and what they could count on. They didn't usually articulate any of that,

unless it was after 10 p.m.—a time I associated more with sleepwalking than soul-searching. But those late-night conversations gave me glimpses into the grief my children were carrying. After a difficult conversation that morphed into an argument, one child shared that she'd lost trust in everyone, not just her dad. As she was talking, I glimpsed the pain she was holding inside. Later, I found out that my other child stayed awake at night, terrified of a break-in, planning an escape route for all of us. She felt we were all vulnerable and spent hours figuring out how to keep us safe. I wish I'd known, so that we could have talked it through.

It might be helpful to think through what's happening in your children's worlds. Consider asking them about what's been hard and what their fears are. And be willing to share yours, as appropriate, if it helps open the door. Their answers may come out slowly but take their concerns seriously. Don't dismiss or rush to fix their fears or try to put a "positivity" spin on them. I've found it's so much better to acknowledge their struggles first and then work together to find ways to help.

SLOW TO SPEAK

Most of us want to pass on what we've learned to our children. Or at least I did. Strangely, they rarely appreciated my liberally offered pearls of wisdom. I learned to choose my moments and not overwhelm them with words. My actions and responses mattered far more than my advice—it really is true that more is caught than taught.

More than well-meaning suggestions, my children needed encouragement. Too often I focused on what they were doing wrong and how I wanted them to turn out rather than on what they were doing well and what they needed. A counselor once reminded me, "Your kids aren't your

products." That stuck. My job wasn't to fix their flaws but to foster their growth.

The older our children are, the more careful we need to be about offering advice. I found that it's best to listen more than I speak and to acknowledge their struggles, and I rarely offer my perspective without being asked first. Unsolicited wisdom usually lands about as well as an invitation to "catch up" from someone selling essential oils—it's well-intentioned but clearly going somewhere you don't want to!

SLOW TO ANGER

We've talked about anger already, but we need to do so again because anger is contagious. My anger sparked the children's and vice versa, creating a downward spiral—especially when I insisted on being right, demanded respect over relationship, or enforced rules without offering grace. Yet when I humbled myself, admitted where I was wrong, and sought restoration, the walls came down. Changing my tone and responding with gentleness, balancing truth with grace, proved far more powerful than reacting with anger or rigid discipline.

As my children have gotten older, they have talked about some of the ways they were hurt through the divorce, including things I could have done differently. While everything in me wanted to defend myself, I was able to listen and apologize, which allowed them to open up and ultimately brought great healing. So, if in the future your children are willing to revisit things, then, if you can, allow them to express their frustration about mistakes you made without being defensive.

SUPPORTING THEIR WORLD

At one time, our family of four had felt like a stable chair with four solid legs. When my daughters' dad left, our life

together suddenly felt wobbly and uncertain. My sister gave me a helpful perspective: think of your family as a three-legged stool. It can still be stable, but it won't look the same.

Maintaining many of our past traditions without their father felt like a painful reminder of what we'd all lost. So we talked about what traditions we wanted to keep, what things we wanted to change, and how we could create new memories. We each offered what was most important to us.

For one child, family vacations were essential. The first year after her dad left, I couldn't manage it, but the next year we went on a cruise. It was something I could handle physically and gave us new collective memories. I also started watching TV shows they enjoyed—something I normally wouldn't do—and made different plans for holidays to avoid focusing on what was missing. On the holidays when I wasn't with them, I made plans in advance so I'd know what I was doing too.

It's worth saying that you don't have to juggle every ball or keep your kids in all the same activities they were in before. It's okay to let some things go. Ask God for the wisdom to know what to release and the strength to handle what remains—he will provide it.

Several families consistently invited my daughters into their homes, including them as part of their family, which made them feel more normal. Having a home-cooked meal with everyone sitting around the table, laughing and talking as we once did, made them feel that they belonged: that they were seen and loved, not just projects to be fixed. On the flip side, my daughters felt invisible, and even as if they were burdens, when well-meaning friends took them aside and told them that their job was to make my life easier, not more difficult.

Counseling was beneficial for me, so I offered it to my daughters as well. Honestly, it led to mixed results then. Now, as adults, they've found counseling helpful and have sought it out on their own. You might prayerfully consider the best ways to support your children, no matter their age, whether through mentoring, counseling, or simply creating space for them to feel loved.

NAVIGATING PARENTING WITH YOUR EX

Navigating the relationship between my ex and my children was bumpy at times. I wanted to help them go through the divorce with as little pain and baggage as possible, which meant being positive about their father. They were figuring out life with their dad and how it would look on an ongoing basis, while I was figuring out my new life without him. Here are a few things I learned along the way...

PARENTING FROM A DISTANCE

For some, the pain isn't just in parenting through divorce—it's in parenting from a distance. If you only see your kids on weekends, during summers, or in the holidays, it may feel like you're missing out on the ordinary moments that build relationships. Maybe your ex has made it difficult for you to stay involved, or your children have pulled away. That's a particularly agonizing kind of heartbreak. I know parents who long for more time with their kids but feel powerless to change their situation.

If that's you, know this: your presence still matters. The moments you do have—whether in person, over the phone, or through texts—are opportunities to build trust. Your children need to know that you love them, that you're still there, and that you're not giving up on them. Pray for wisdom in how to use those moments well, even when

your child feels distant. Don't give up. Something is always better than nothing, and the Lord can use what feels like a little to accomplish a lot.

DON'T SABOTAGE THEIR RELATIONSHIP WITH YOUR EX

At first I was tempted to share negative things about their dad with my daughters. It wasn't that I wanted to badmouth him constantly, but when my kids praised him or repeated his criticisms of me, I wanted to slip in a few jabs of my own or correct what he had said and offer my version of the truth. Yet I knew the high road was worth taking. I needed to guard what I said for the good of my daughters.

Every day, I would read a note I'd pinned to my bulletin board: "Faith is trusting God to set the record straight." I knew that it would be best for our children if they had a good relationship with their father rather than a fractured, mistrustful one. My perspective would shape their ideas of him (and of men in general), so I didn't point out their dad's faults. As they grew older, they would understand and see each of our strengths and weaknesses.

Both my daughters have thanked me years later for not speaking negatively about their dad. After seeing their dad one weekend, one texted, "I never once heard you say anything bad about Dad, and I know that helped my relationship with him. Thank you."

If you've got into a habit of criticizing your ex to your kids, it's not too late to change course. Simply stopping now will make a difference, but you could also acknowledge what's happened by saying, "I realize I haven't always spoken about your dad (or mom) in the best way. I'm sorry about my careless words, and I want to do better." Owning it models humility and keeps your children from feeling they have to choose sides.

CONSIDER WHAT'S BEST FOR THEM

I didn't share details about the divorce with my kids when they were younger, and even as they became adults, I only shared what they wanted to know. No matter what happens, my ex will always be their father, and whatever I say about him will stick in their minds.

That said, admittedly I wanted my kids to love me more than my ex. To choose me. To want to be with me. But I knew that putting them in the middle would only hurt them, so I tried not to make them feel guilty for spending time with their dad.

My ex was more lenient than I was, which often made me the stricter parent. I heard plenty of "Dad lets us do ___. Why don't you?" which was infuriating, especially when it related to issues that we'd both agreed on in the past, such as watching particular movies, setting spending limits, and limiting screen time. I had to let go of managing everything, knowing that he was handling things differently than I was. (That said, if any type of abuse is or might be involved, parents need to be aware of everything that happens when the children are with the other parent. If that's the case, do all you can do to protect your children, praying for them even as you are embroiled in custody and court battles.)

IT'S A LONG GAME

When I was despairing over my daughters, a mentor said, "Parenting is a long game. Don't judge the end by what you see now." I needed to hear that, and if you're struggling with your children, I want you to hear that too. And where you've made mistakes, there's always a chance to repair. Just be willing to listen, admit when you've failed, and ask for forgiveness.

Though we all long for our children to flourish and walk with God, that can't be our the yardstick for assessing how

we're doing in our parenting. They will make their own choices, some of which may bring heartache, but their decisions are not a measure of our worth or faithfulness as parents. We often judge our parenting by outcomes, but God doesn't—he simply calls us to be faithful. He knows our limits, strengthens us for what he asks, and offers mercy when we fall short.

Today I'm remarkably close to my daughters, partly because of what we went through together. One of them recently wrote this:

> *"You were the best mom for us— not because you did everything perfectly but because you showed us Christ. I watched you faithfully walk through everything with Dad, and I realized there is no way you could've done that on your own. Thank you for showing us Christ every day."*

That letter, those words, made it all worth it. Well, almost.

CHAPTER 7

THE CHURCH, THE CROWD, AND THE FRIENDS WHO STAYED

I was crushingly lonely after my divorce. There were few people I could confide in, and fewer still who could handle the messy realities of my new life.

After my ex left, I wrote in my journal:

> *"I am so lonely. Gut-level lonely. Lonely like I've never been before. Right after [he] left, people called all the time just to check in. Now no one calls to check in. They assume I'm fine, and they go on with their lives. They have their families and their own things to do. I get it.*
>
> *"I can laugh and talk to my friends, but somehow I feel no one knows me anymore. I want a sense of belonging. To know and be known. The pain is so deep, and the emptiness feels tangible, but it doesn't feel safe to open my heart to anyone. Does anyone really care? Or really know me?"*

Maybe you can relate to those feelings. It wasn't that I didn't have friends, but I had layers of complication that few people could relate to. Crawling into an empty bed at night only deepened that ache.

I needed to find my place—a new place. At first, I kept reaching for the things I'd always leaned on, but they weren't there anymore. Slowly, I began to discover the beauty of solitude, the grounding truth of my identity in Christ, and the richness of new community. I found my place again—in church, in friendships, and in the faithful presence of God.

LONELINESS VERSUS SOLITUDE

At first, being alone felt the same as being lonely. But as I looked around, I noticed plenty of single people living fulfilled, vibrant lives. To get there, I had to change how I viewed myself—not as someone rejected, uninteresting, or unworthy but as someone valuable, vibrant, and content with my own company.

When my ex first left, I filled my weekend nights with plans so I'd stay busy while our daughters were with him. But one Saturday night, I had nothing scheduled. When I realized I'd be alone, I called ten people. Most didn't answer, and the few who did were busy. No one even had time for a quick conversation. When I hung up after the last call, I broke down sobbing. Why didn't anyone ever ask me to do anything on weekend nights? With nowhere else to turn, I went into my prayer closet and poured my heart out to God. As I did, I realized I wasn't alone; God was with me.

The rest of the evening felt different, and for the first time I was truly okay being alone.

I used to think solitude was just solitary confinement with better lighting and snacks. But in the quiet, I realized I could better hear God's voice. When I was alone, I began to

discover who I was beyond the noise. I filled my time with things I enjoyed: reading the Bible, watercolor painting, journaling, or getting lost in a good book. Choosing to be alone felt different than being left out. It felt freeing.

SHAME AND IDENTITY

Shame felt like a shadow that followed me after my divorce. Since few people knew the details, I imagined everyone was speculating about what I had done wrong. Some days I wondered the same thing as I went over every detail of what I did and didn't do, berating myself for every little misstep.

But shame runs deeper than quirks or mistakes because shame isn't really about what we've done—it's about who we believe we are.

Brené Brown, a leading researcher on shame, defines shame as "the intensely painful feeling or experience of believing that we are flawed and therefore unworthy of love and belonging."[16] That perfectly describes how I felt after my separation. I believed the cruel lies that my shame whispered about my worth: *You're not enough. You've failed. You're marked by this forever.*

I felt a misplaced sense of shame because of what had happened to me, believing my ex's rejection was a reflection of my value. Biblical counselor and author Ed Welch explains:

> *"More often shame is not so much a result of what you have done but of what was done to you. When you are treated as nothing, you will feel like nothing. When you are treated disgracefully, you believe you are a disgrace."*[17]

That sums up where I was.

---

16 Brené Brown, "Shame vs. Guilt," brenebrown.com, brenebrown.com/articles/2013/01/15/shame-v-guilt/ (accessed April 15, 2025).

17 Edward Welch, *A Small Book About Why We Hide* (New Growth Press, 2021), p. 4.

Other Christians might also unintentionally deepen our feelings of misplaced shame. Married men sometimes worry that their wives might pick up "wrong ideas" from divorced friends. Women can steer their husbands away from conversations with divorced friends, afraid that they could lead to flirtation. Even couples tend to keep their distance, as if divorce is somehow contagious. The unspoken assumptions are often the hardest to bear. Like Job's friends, some assume that if you're divorced, you must be at fault. They convince themselves that divorce doesn't happen to faithful people.

If you feel the sting of shame, remember that you are loved by God, and he alone defines your worth. Your identity is in Christ, not in what happened to you or what others assume about you.

Of course, you may be reading this knowing you played a significant role in causing your divorce. Maybe you regret choices you made, and your shame is justified. If that's you, take heart—God's grace is for you too. The cross covers every sin, every failure, and every broken promise. You do need to repent. But when you repent, know that "if we confess our sins, he is faithful and just to forgive us our sins and to cleanse us from all unrighteousness" (1 John 1:9). Your past doesn't define you. Christ's forgiveness is real, and his mercy runs deeper than your worst mistakes.

Shame does not need to define you. Christ's love can.

THE CHURCH: HURT AND HEALING

HOW THE CHURCH CAN HURT

Churches can, unwittingly, make divorced people feel like outsiders. One Sunday after the service, I mentioned to the person beside me that I was writing this book. She whispered, "I was divorced years ago from an abusive

husband, but I don't share it much because I don't know how people will respond." It broke my heart to realize how judged she had felt before.

I'm thankful my pastor and elders supported me through my divorce, though I know that's not the case for everyone. Yet even in my church, some people were critical, even telling the pastor that I was no longer qualified to teach Bible study. I'm grateful that he wanted me to keep leading. But there are some ministries and churches who believe that being divorced alone disqualifies people from serving—as if someone's marital status makes them unfit for ministry.

Though I felt supported by my church leadership, some Christians said and did hurtful things, often asking inappropriate questions: *Was your divorce biblical? Were you submissive enough? How did you contribute to the failure?* I have friends who endured unspeakable marital abuse, who were then asked to share the details to prove it was "really abuse." Those questions made the wounds deeper, confirming my friends' fears that they would be blamed. Abuse is never a marriage problem; abuse is a sin problem. Yet some seem determined to turn the situation around and shoot the wounded, putting more effort into trying to restore the sinner than caring for the one who had been hurt.

One friend, whose husband was abusive and unfaithful, wrote a letter to her church elders explaining her situation. No one ever responded. She had been actively involved in the church, but when she needed their support the most, they were silent. It seemed easier for them to ignore the problem than to deal with it.

With experiences like that, it is understandable that some wonder why they should bother with church at all.

WHY WE NEED THE CHURCH

Despite its flaws, the church is where God meets his people. "Let us consider how to stir up one another to love and good works," Hebrews 10:24-25 reminds us, "not neglecting to meet together, as is the habit of some, but encouraging one another, and all the more as you see the Day drawing near." While I wanted to stay in bed and pull the covers over my head after my ex left, I knew I needed to be in church. Gathering for worship encouraged me as I sang the words I needed to remember. Sermons stirred me as the Holy Spirit spoke directly to my circumstances. Fellowship, both after the service and in small groups, gave me hope when I felt weary. We were going through 1 Peter in women's Bible study, which felt tailor-made for me.

Attending church in person, despite the awkwardness or potential judgment, keeps us rooted in truth. When our prayers seemingly go unanswered, we need others to remind us of God's faithfulness. We can ask them to pray for us when we have no words ourselves and to support us when we find our faith wavering. Kelly Kapic puts it this way:

> *"The saints speak to God for us when we struggle to believe and speak alone. Further, the saints are called to speak to us for God when we seem unable to hear him on our own. Their prayers sustain our faith; their proclamation reignites our hope."*[18]

We are all part of the family of God: "You are the body of Christ and individually members of it" (1 Corinthians 12:27). Without that connection with other believers, it's easy to drift. We may have once burned brightly for God,

---

18 Kelly Kapic, *Embodied Hope: A Theological Meditation on Pain and Suffering* (IVP Academic, 2017), p. 128.

like an ember in a roaring fire, but when removed from the warmth of community, we eventually flicker out and grow cold.

The church is full of broken people, but God still works through it to keep us close to him and to make us more like him. Don't give up on the body of Christ, even when it's hard. Through the messiness of community, God is shaping us—you and others—into the image of Christ.

BUT CHURCH CAN BE… DIFFICULT

Walking into church as a divorced person was daunting. I'd always gone to church with my husband, so sitting without him, I felt conspicuous and lonely. Seeing happy, intact families all around, with kids carrying their highlighted Bibles as they attentively took notes, made me want to launch a paper airplane straight at their perfect little heads. Conveniently, my daughters had already turned their bulletins into an air force.

I remember one Easter when my daughters invited some friends to church. I saved eight seats near the front, placing bulletins and a sweater to mark them. As the church filled, people asked if the seats were taken, and I assured them my family was coming. But my daughters never showed up. They had decided to sit with another family, so I eventually let latecomers take the seats as I sheepishly removed the bulletins. Later, my daughters admitted that they didn't want to sit with me because we didn't feel like a family anymore.

For a while, my children had been feeling conspicuous in church, aware that we looked different from other families. It felt especially obvious when the room was full. With so few divorced families, we often felt that a spotlight was on us. After my daughter overheard her friends talking about our family in the bathroom, church

didn't feel safe to her anymore. We later talked about how hard that was, but I couldn't "fix it" for them. Their identity had changed too.

You may struggle to find your place in church. Singles groups may not feel like the right fit, but you're likely not comfortable in groups geared to married couples either. With limited time and energy, it's tempting to stop attending altogether. If you're feeling this way, reflect on what would help you stay connected. If your small group feels awkward, try joining a new one. If sitting alone in the service feels uncomfortable, ask a friend to save you a seat. If you're looking for fellowship, plan a lunch after church with someone. And if your schedule allows, consider volunteering at church, which is a great way to both serve and to build community.

If you've stepped away from your church because you've been wounded or unsupported, I'm so sorry that happened. But please don't give up on the church altogether. Perhaps consider talking to the leadership about what you've experienced or finding another place to worship. I know it will be hard to walk through the door of a new church, so perhaps ask a friend to go with you. You could also watch an online service first, to get a sense of the church's atmosphere. If you do visit a new church, know that you don't owe anyone an explanation for your singleness, so don't feel pressured to answer intrusive questions. But if you want to have something prepared beforehand, you could simply say, "I'm recently divorced, and it's been a hard journey. I'm leaning on the Lord and taking it one day at a time." If you feel that the church is a good fit, it might be helpful to meet with a pastor, the person who oversees discipleship ministry, or, if you're a woman, someone in women's ministry. Ask if they have members who are divorced or widowed or how they handle single

parents. They may not have specific ministries geared to single adults, but letting them know about your situation can help you figure out where to connect.

A MORE POWERFUL TESTIMONY

It's easy to feel that your testimony has been ruined by your divorce. Maybe you thought that trusting Christ as your Savior would lead to a successful life marked by a thriving marriage, faith-filled children, and a flourishing career. Now your story is... complicated.

My daughter attended a middle-school basketball camp where the leader promised prosperity to everyone who was willing to raise their hand and commit their life to Jesus. I left that meeting in tears. I was a single mom, trying to hold life together. I already felt like a failure, and that declaration sealed it. My testimony didn't seem welcome there.

Yet now, years later, I've had more opportunities to share about the sufficiency of Christ through my divorce than I ever did through my "happy family."

Your divorce, with all its pain and heartache, can be a powerful way to live out the gospel. Even without sharing your story, your faithfulness in suffering speaks volumes. Simply clinging to Christ, showing up at church, and saying, "This is hard, but I'm trusting Jesus," is a beautiful and compelling testimony in itself. Remember, most people aren't watching to judge—they're looking for hope. And your quiet perseverance may encourage more people than you realize.

The gospel is about God's faithfulness, not our righteousness or the success of our lives. When we see perfect families worshiping in church, we want their lives. But when we see broken families trusting the Lord, we want their God. Sharing your story of God's faithfulness

amid shattered dreams may be the greatest witness you could ever offer.

WHEN WE NEED COMMUNITY

God wired us to need other people. In the Garden of Eden, though Adam had perfect fellowship with the trinitarian God, God still wanted him to have human companionship. He said, "It is not good that the man should be alone; I will make him a helper fit for him" (Genesis 2:18). God designed us for human connection, to help each other, to know and be known.

But that often becomes harder when you're walking through divorce.

Immediately after my ex left, friendships felt different. Though I didn't move, the people around me changed and some relationships shifted. My conversations with my in-laws were strained at first, and I know several friends who were cut off from their in-laws after their marriage dissolved. It was painful to lose relationships that were once central to my life—to grow distant from people I loved and trusted.

Community felt messier than I expected. I was surprised at the unsolicited feedback I received about every aspect of my life. While many didn't voice criticism, people seemed more distant, dinner parties happened without me, and I felt as if I'd missed the group text—assuming there even was one. When I did get invited, I felt like the awkward third or fifth wheel, second-guessing whether I was fun or interesting enough to get another invitation. Some made a concerted effort at first but soon moved on with their lives, assuming that I was fine. As one friend of mine who has walked through this summed it up, "Post-divorce community is SO hard—it fundamentally shifts everything. All your ecosystems change. Some friends

treat divorce like a 'timestamp' suffering, thinking you'll move on." As you know, the fallout from divorce is more widespread than anyone would expect.

How do we navigate the challenges of community, especially when we've been hurt? I used to dwell on all the ways people failed to show up for me, but that only made me feel more isolated. I saw that though Job's friends berated him at his lowest point, God ultimately wanted Job to pray for them (Job 42:8). It's amazing how praying for someone can make us feel less bitter towards them.

It took effort and initiative to rebuild my support system, and when I did, I found that single friends were easier to connect with on weekends. To expand my circle, I also started inviting people I didn't know that well to have coffee, asking the Lord to show me who to call. At first I didn't want to develop a thriving community as a single person, but my counselor kept telling me that my worth did not depend on me getting married again, and remarriage wasn't something to put my life on hold for.

As I shared earlier in the book, I leaned too heavily on one friend I'd known for years, expecting more from her than she could give. I forgot that she had her own life and challenges and couldn't always be available when I needed her. Years later, we finally talked about our expectations and how we had both felt unseen at times. That honest conversation was so helpful—I only wish we'd had the courage to have it sooner.

Proximity played a big role in my relationships. People I saw regularly offered to do more than others I didn't see as frequently. That might be true for you as well, as neighbors, coworkers and other nearby acquaintances may become a bigger part of your support system than you might have expected. I often crossed paths during drop-offs and pick-ups with one mom whose daughter was close

friends with mine. She stepped up when others didn't, offering practical help and inviting me out for coffee dates. Since we already saw each other several times a week, checking in felt more natural.

You'll find two simple forms in the appendices—one to help you share your needs and one for friends to indicate how they might be able to support you. They aren't meant to create guilt or obligation, but just to make communication clearer in a hard season. But even as you ask for help, remember that friends will inevitably disappoint. Only Jesus won't. Let others reflect his love, but don't expect them to replace it.

I mentioned in chapter 3 that a close friend created a text thread with four women, including me, to support her through her divorce. We didn't all know each other, but we all wanted to support her. She described the group this way: "They gave me advice on emails and texts I needed to send. What stands out is that they let me feel everything I needed to feel without judgment but helped me stop wrong thinking that wouldn't lead to healing." I loved being part of that circle and was thankful that, since someone was usually available, no one person felt pressured to respond immediately (in contrast to my kids, who generally expect me to respond to a text a nanosecond after they've hit send).

Who you choose to invest in matters deeply. Prioritize hearing from those who will point you toward the Lord. What you take in—whether it's advice from friends, books, or social media—will have a tremendous impact on you, especially now, when many of your support systems feel shaky.

When you look at your friendships, how do you feel? If married friends have drifted away, you might consider saying, "I realize we haven't been getting together as much

because we used to do things as couples. I'd love to find another way to connect." Being honest can sometimes salvage and strengthen relationships that might otherwise fade away. Even so, you may end up feeling disappointed that some people simply haven't shown up for you. It's worth remembering that some people feel inadequate or overwhelmed by their own challenges. Their distance probably isn't a judgment on you, and it doesn't need to feel personal.

If you want to widen your circle, volunteering can be a fulfilling way to do that. Nonprofits are always looking for volunteers, which could help distract you from your own problems for a while. I highly recommend going to DivorceCare, a program for people walking through divorce, which is offered in many US cities and many countries worldwide. There you can connect with people who are going through similar challenges. For me, seeing people at different stages of healing gave me hope that I would make it through.

FIND YOUR ONESIPHORUS

I needed faithful friends through my divorce, similar to the way Paul longed to be remembered when he was in prison. He said:

> *You are aware that all who are in Asia turned away from me ... May the Lord grant mercy to the household of Onesiphorus, for he often refreshed me and was not ashamed of my chains, but when he arrived in Rome he searched for me earnestly and found me.*
>
> *(2 Timothy 1:15-17)*

Like Paul, I felt deserted when friends pulled away unexpectedly. I love the way that Onesiphorus did the opposite. He sought Paul out, unashamed of Paul's

situation, and offered the support that Paul longed for. We all want friends like that: who'll check in, support us, and genuinely care how we're doing. It's significant that it wasn't a crowd who supported Paul but one loyal friend.

For me, that friend was my sister. She consistently picked up the phone, listened to my tears, made me laugh, and believed in me when I didn't believe in myself. She encouraged me in my faith, empathized with my struggles, and held me accountable. Another friend stepped in as well and helped me rethink my priorities. She suggested I drop some draining activities that I'd doggedly stayed committed to. I resisted at first, but taking her advice led to wiser choices. I was grateful that she recognized what was depleting me and was willing to challenge me.

As you think about the people you interact with and trust, prayerfully consider identifying one or two with whom you can meet regularly to pray, share your concerns, and encourage one another. You may need to ask several people before someone is able to do that, so please don't get discouraged and give up. Expect to run into roadblocks because initiating and planning takes effort, while vulnerability takes time. But a relationship like that is worth pursuing. Everyone needs an Onesiphorus when life is hard.

Of course, no friend is perfect. They have their own struggles, their own chaos, their own late-night Google searches about whether their car is about to explode. They'll be busy when we need them, say the wrong thing, or fall short in ways that sting. So will we. Relationships last when friends show up for each other and friends forgive each other, rather than when one does all the giving and listening or when either demands perfection from the other. So even when we're struggling, it's

important to check in on friends too—and to cut them some slack when we feel they've not been there for us. If you aren't sure how to get to the next level with your friends, perhaps consider discussing these seven thoughtful questions from counseling pastor and author Brad Hambrick:

1. What's your story?
2. What's good?
3. What's hard?
4. What's bad?
5. What's fun?
6. Where are you stuck?
7. What's next?[19]

Healing often starts with small, brave steps: sending that text, showing up even when it's awkward, or saying yes to an invitation. Churches may struggle to provide perfect support, but it's in personal friendships, both in and outside the church, where you'll often feel most seen and understood. As Ed Welch says:

> *"Friends are the best helpers. They come prepackaged with compassion and love. All they need is wisdom, and that is available to everyone."*[20]

And you can not only lean on those kind of friends; you can be that kind of friend. Through all you've gone through, you now know the struggles of divorce firsthand

---

19 Brad Hambrick, *Transformative Friendships: 7 Questions to Deepen Any Relationship* (New Growth Press, 2024).

20 Edward Welch, *Side by Side: Walking with Others in Wisdom and Love* (Crossway, 2015), p. 13.

and will be able to show up for others with grace, empathy, and wisdom. In the quiet strength of friendship, you can begin to rebuild—not just a life but a sense of belonging in the unfamiliar terrain of life after divorce.

CHAPTER 8

DATING AND THE R WORD

This is a shorter chapter than the others. In one sense it doesn't "fit" in the flow of this book—it is one you might not be in a position to read yet, or you may have no desire to read it at all. Equally it may be a chapter you turned straight to.

It's the one about dating and remarriage.

Remarriage after divorce is a much-debated topic in the church. Thoughtful Christians have long wrestled with it, just as they have with the question of divorce itself. And just as this book doesn't offer a definitive stance on when divorce is biblically permitted, it also doesn't give advice on when remarriage is appropriate. This is something each person must bring before the Lord, carefully considering what the Bible says.

I encourage you to pray about it, search the Scriptures (including those I mentioned in chapter 1—see pages 22-23), read from a range of perspectives, and talk with your pastor or someone on staff at your church. In an appendix I've included several books and articles that

present different viewpoints to help you think through the issue. Faithful Christians don't all land in the same place here, so it's important to approach the conversation with humility and grace toward those who hold different views. But don't avoid the issue—take the time to explore it biblically and prayerfully.

You might find this section, or even this whole chapter, difficult. You may be thinking that remarriage is a good option for you to hope for or pursue—or you may be feeling otherwise. For those of us who have walked through divorce, these conversations can feel intensely personal. I remember times that the topic came up and all I wanted to do was cry. I already felt judged, and the discussion only deepened my sense of shame and disqualification.

If that's where you are, I understand those feelings. But I also want to encourage you not to take this lightly. After prayer, study, and seeking wise counsel, I became convinced that for me remarriage was consistent with Scripture. My goal isn't to persuade you toward a particular conclusion but to encourage you to seek God's wisdom as you consider what comes next.

Early on after my divorce, being honest, the reason why I wanted to heal quickly was so that I could remarry. I assumed that being married again was the only way I could be happy. My counselor encouraged me to build healthy friendships and find contentment where I was, rather than putting my life on hold until I found a husband. I didn't love that idea at first. But she kept emphasizing that her clients who were solely focused on remarrying often made poor choices—choices they later regretted.

She was right.

I'll never forget running into an old friend at the dentist's office. She had recently remarried and leaned

over to whisper, "I heard you just got divorced, and I wanted to give you one piece of advice. Don't remarry too quickly." We moved on to small talk, but those words stayed with me.

I know that the pressure to find someone, and to do so quickly, can feel overwhelming, especially when you're lonely. That sense of urgency may come from wanting to have children or to have another parent in the home or to simply avoid being alone. It's natural to long to feel loved and wanted again, so I totally understand the desire to start dating.

But don't let your emotions lead you into unwise decisions with people who "fit the bill"—as in, who are breathing and available. You need time to emotionally heal and rediscover yourself first—and jumping into a new relationship will not hurry that process along. What will help most is first focusing on rediscovering yourself, becoming aware of your strengths and weaknesses.

WHAT WON'T I COMPROMISE?

We've been exploring priorities throughout this book, and one way to bring those ideas together is to create a personal mission statement. I realize that a mission statement is a business term, but don't dismiss it too quickly. The process of drafting it will help you think through your core values and determine what you won't compromise. Here are two examples:

- *To grow deeper in my relationship with Christ, build a community that reflects his love, and pursue healing as I live a life of integrity and purpose.*
- *To authentically live my faith, cultivate joy in the small things, and remain open to the unexpected blessings of this new season as I trust God's plan for my future.*

To create your own mission statement, consider blocking out time to reflect on what's most important to you. Brainstorm ideas, values, and where you want to be headed. After you write your mission out, place it somewhere visible to you. It can be a daily reminder to stay anchored in truth, guiding you as you navigate decisions about your future including relationships, whether it be singleness, dating, or remarriage.

Referring to your mission statement will make sure your choices align with your values.

Before I started dating, my counselor and I spent time exploring why I wanted to remarry. Was it for companionship or healing, or to escape loneliness? How would it impact my daughters, and were they ready for that transition? What qualities did I value in a partner, and what boundaries would I set? We talked about timing, how I might meet people, and whether remarriage was even something I should pursue. So if you are interested in getting remarried at some point, think through those questions. And if you're not yet ready for remarriage, ask yourself whether you're truly ready to date. Seek counsel from a wise friend or mentor: someone who knows you well and loves you enough to be honest even when you disagree. Remember that there is nothing wrong with remaining single; you're not missing anything or falling short. But if you do begin dating, approach it prayerfully and cautiously.

So, with all that said, here are my five pieces of practical advice for dating as a divorced person.

1. KEEP CHRIST FIRST – THEN DON'T SETTLE FOR LESS

Prioritize finding someone who is walking with Christ, whose love for the Lord is evident by the way they live.

Scripture is clear that our closest relationships should encourage us in faith, not pull us away. Paul is very clear: "Do not be unequally yoked with unbelievers. For what partnership has righteousness with lawlessness? Or what fellowship has light with darkness?" (2 Corinthians 6:14). It can be tempting, especially after divorce, to settle for less out of fear that no one godly will come along. Please don't do that. Be willing to wait for someone who truly loves Jesus because he is what matters most.

You don't need to decide after every date if you could marry that person—that's way too much pressure. Instead, focus on getting to know them and how they make you feel. Don't be so concerned about impressing someone that you overlook your own instincts. If you have any hesitations, trust your gut. Take your time and let your emotions settle before making decisions.

2. PAY ATTENTION TO BOUNDARIES AND RED FLAGS

Establish boundaries to protect your heart and honor your convictions. Decide ahead of time what your boundaries are, share them with a trusted friend, and ask them to hold you accountable. If someone pressures you to cross those boundaries, it's a clear sign they aren't worth pursuing. Being faithful to the Lord is your top priority; as Peter warns us, we're to "be diligent to be found by him without spot or blemish [and] take care that you are not carried away with the error of lawless people and lose your own stability" (2 Peter 3:14,17). Being pressured to compromise your convictions won't just cloud your judgment—it will begin to pull you into the very drift Peter warns against.

Watch for red flags: if you find yourself hiding details about the relationship because you feel ashamed or "others

wouldn't understand," or if the person you're dating asks (outright or by aggressively hinting) to borrow money, you likely need to step back. Healthy relationships thrive on trust, mutual respect, and accountability rather than secrecy or manipulation.

Even the smallest red flag deserves your attention. If something's tugging at you or making you feel uneasy, don't dismiss it, hoping it will go away. Bring it into the light when it surfaces, because once emotions or attraction take hold, it's easy to lose perspective. Keep asking the Lord for discernment through prayer and the counsel of others. Make sure your friends have met the person you're dating and take their feedback seriously as you consider who this person is, not who you hope they'll become.

3. BE CAUTIOUS WITH DATING APPS

Online dating was not what I'd call a dream. Frankly, it felt as exhausting as working the midnight shift after a long day. I've never heard anyone, ever, say, "I love online dating." That said, I met my husband, Joel, on a dating app, so I can't bash the whole thing outright. But let's be real—the process was... excruciating. Not with him, of course, but the journey to find him felt like one long, awkward episode of *The Twilight Zone*.

Putting together a profile was like selling myself on Facebook Marketplace: "Gently used, slightly over-caffeinated, comes with a love of Jesus and sarcasm. Only serious offers, please." I just prayed someone decent would like me—and that they wouldn't turn out to be a serial killer. Or a scam artist. Or both.

Thankfully, I managed to dodge those bullets, but misrepresentation by "Christians" was disturbingly common on dating apps. Few people posted photos that

even resembled themselves. It was as if they'd unearthed some decades-old glamor shots and had decided to upload those, hoping that no one would notice. Their write-ups made them sound as if they were up for the Mother Teresa Memorial Award, which didn't quite match reality.

For example, there was the guy who proudly told me over coffee that his favorite book was *Fifty Shades of Grey*. (Yes, I finished my latte, but barely.) Then there was the guy who ghosted me—only for his wife to reach out later and inform me he was married. And how could I forget the gentleman who hired a babysitter for his cat when he worked, and even during our dinner date, not to mention the profile pictures featuring bare-chested selfies of guys cuddling on the couch with their cat. Some things you just wish you could "unsee."

My husband had his own share of online dating pitfalls. Many of the women were decades older than their profiles suggested. One date spent the entire evening detailing the raw sewage problem in her bathroom, leaving Joel to wonder if she was secretly hoping he was a plumber. (He isn't.)

That said, online dating can be a helpful way to meet people. If you decide to try it, go in with clear eyes and realistic expectations. You might meet someone deep and grounded… or someone whose hamster sees a therapist on the regular. Be prayerfully discerning—everyone is trying to make a good impression, but their lives may not match what they say. Regardless of what others do, don't stretch the truth about who you are. Don't airbrush your life or your photos. Be a person of integrity. Stay anchored in truth, keep praying, and remember—your worth isn't defined by someone's interest in your profile.

4. RECOGNIZE YOUR WORTH

I was determined not to meet someone with baggage—until my sister reminded me, "You're not exactly carry-on luggage yourself." She wasn't wrong. I wasn't everyone's dream date, but I wanted to be. Rejection felt personal, and after many Saturday nights alone, I kept wondering what was wrong with me. Looking back, I wish I hadn't tied my self-worth to being chosen.

I had to constantly remind myself that I was enough, regardless of whether some random guy liked my profile. If you're feeling discouraged by a lack of dating success, let me tell you what I wish I'd heard and, more importantly, what I wish I'd believed: you are fearfully and wonderfully made by the God of the universe, the cross tells you how much he loves you, and every day he delights in you. His love is unwavering, and that is what defines you.

If you've dated for a while and haven't met anyone you'd consider marrying, lowering your standards may start to look appealing. My sister's husband kept telling me not to settle just because I hadn't found the right person yet. He was right—not because I was particularly special, but because I was already whole in Christ. I didn't need a relationship to prove my worth, and neither do you.

Your value isn't in being chosen by someone on a dating app (or anywhere else)—it's in being chosen by Jesus. You don't need a relationship to be complete. You are already complete in Christ.

5. TRUST GOD

As I mentioned, I met my husband on a dating app. By the time I'd met him, I had been on quite a few dates with other people and hadn't found anyone I could imagine spending my life with. Frustrated, I decided to stop looking altogether. But providentially, on the very day I

went to deactivate my profile, I met Joel.

Joel has been an immeasurable gift in my life, and I am beyond thankful for him. But my life isn't whole or fulfilled just because I met Joel. It is whole and fulfilled because I know Jesus. Single, divorced, married, or remarried, Jesus is the one who brings joy to our life. So wherever you are in your thinking on dating, I want to underscore that you don't need to get remarried to be happy.

The apostle Paul saw singleness as a gift. He encouraged those who were unmarried—or released from marriage—not to rush into a new relationship but to see singleness as an opportunity to serve the Lord without distraction (1 Corinthians 7:7-8, 27, 32). I have friends who haven't remarried and who, like Paul, have found joy in friendships, church, and meaningful pursuits. Singleness is not a consolation prize. It can be a rich, rewarding season, or a beautiful, lifelong calling. These friends have embraced deep friendships, vibrant church communities, and fulfilling work, and have purposeful, joy-filled lives. If you're longing to be married, I recognize that you may feel a deep ache because God hasn't brought someone into your life. I felt that way for years. But I've learned that contentment doesn't come from getting everything I want. Contentment comes from trusting God with what I have, and believing he is enough.

As you look back on your mission statement, I hope you will continue to make choices that align with your values. It that can be a great way to evaluate whether a relationship draws you closer to the life—and the God—you want to pursue. It can keep you grounded, even when the waiting feels long.

In that waiting, remember this: "Your Maker is your husband, the LORD of hosts is his name" (Isaiah 54:5). You

are not forgotten or overlooked. God himself promises to be your faithful companion and provider, offering a love more steadfast than any human relationship could give. He is with you—and he is enough.

CHAPTER 9

HOPE ON THE HORIZON

I began this book describing how the end of my marriage felt like going through a fire. The life I had built was gone, destroyed by flames that spread quickly, leaving little untouched. It was devastating.

But now, looking back, I see that it wasn't a wildfire—it was a controlled burn. The difference is profound. Controlled fires, though painful, are meant for good. Now I can see that truth; I can see that my divorce gave me much more than it took from me.

This poem by Ullie-Kaye beautifully captures what I've learned through the fire. And maybe you're beginning to see that it might reflect your story too:

fires.

and if you have ever been abandoned,
be a constant. if you have ever been
wrapped up in nights so dark, you
could not find your way back home,
be light. if you have ever fallen apart
in a thousand, fractured pieces and
wondered where on earth everyone has

gone, be present. if you have ever felt
unworthy. unbeautiful. unseen. unknown.
unheard. be love. i tell you the truth.
some of the most precious things we learn,
are from the fires that we've endured.

—*ullie-kaye*[21]

Fires are terrifying when they feel close and uncontained. The heat, the loss, the uncertainty—it's all-consuming. Standing in the ashes, I couldn't imagine anything good coming from all the destruction. You may also feel abandoned, lost, and broken in the fire of your divorce. Maybe you are feeling the sting of those dark nights and fractured pieces.

But this is not the end of your story.

You will get through this.

You will become stronger. You will grow in ways you never imagined you would or could. And you will discover that what Satan meant for evil, God will use for good in your life.

We've covered a lot together—grief, bitterness, parenting struggles, and finding hope in the ruins. We've talked about the lies we carry, the beauty of lament, and how healing often looks like small, brave steps rather than sweeping transformations. We've explored the importance of walking in grace, releasing what isn't ours to carry, and daring to dream again. I hope these pages have reminded you that you're not alone and that God has not forgotten you. He is with you, moving in ways you may not yet see.

HEALING AND RESTORATION

I so want you to heal after your divorce—not just superficially but deeply. But it does take time. I wanted

---

21 *Fires: Hardship, Grief and Perseverance*, p. 1.

my healing to be instant, but I learned that healing is not like that. God, in his tenderness, heals the brokenhearted and binds up their wounds (Psalm 147:3) as he draws near to them, so they heal over time. Perhaps that's because healing wounds isn't just about getting rid of the pain—it's also about being changed and growing.

Healing requires that we carefully tend to our wounds and be vigilant to prevent infection. This is why I encouraged you in chapter 3 to start releasing your bitterness. Letting go of bitterness and allowing the wound to heal may mean revisiting the hurt, not to dwell on it but to clean out what might fester. It's messy and slow, but it's worth it. And as with all other wounds, it will likely leave a scar—a mark of survival and strength, and a reminder of God's faithfulness.

Once I realized that healing would take time, I was impatient to know when it would come. I wrestled with God's timing, asking, "How long, O Lord?" Of course, I was not the first to ask this; just read the psalms! The prophet Habakkuk asked the same question too, wondering how long it would be until the Lord rescued his people. God's response was both a challenge and a reassurance: "For still the vision awaits its appointed time; it hastens to the end—it will not lie. If it seems slow, wait for it; it will surely come; it will not delay" (Habakkuk 2:3).

Waiting on God's timing can feel excruciating. There were days when I cried out, "Why is this taking so long?" or "Have you forgotten me?" While clinging to God's promises gave me hope, knowing them didn't take away the pain. The only encouraging part was that, as with my daughters' piano recitals, there was an appointed end. While it seemed slow, it wouldn't be delayed. God's timing is precise, not random, and he will not let us wait even a

moment longer than necessary. In the end, we can be sure that blessing awaits us.

And restoration is part of that blessing. God assured the Israelites, "I will restore to you the years that the swarming locust has eaten" (Joel 2:25, NKJV). The great Victorian preacher Charles Spurgeon explained:

> *"Lost years can never be restored literally. So the meaning of restoration of the years must be the restoration of those fruits and of the harvest the locusts consumed... God can give back all [we] would have had if the locusts had never come. God can restore our lives."*[22]

While the years themselves cannot return, God can abundantly restore us, making sure that nothing has been wasted. Restoration may not look like a return to the life you lost or a perfect ending tied with a bow. Instead, it may come in unexpected, quieter ways—a new community of friends, a deeper relationship with God, a renewed sense of grace and peace.

FAITH IN THE MIDST OF SHATTERED DREAMS

You may be at a crossroads, wondering if God is who he says he is. Your life hasn't turned out the way you planned, and the world may be offering quick solutions that seem better or faster. That's when we are most vulnerable, tempted to doubt God's goodness.

Doubt can feel isolating, but it's part of the journey for many of us. Faith isn't about never doubting; it's about choosing to trust God even when the path feels uncertain.

Satan wants to convince you that God cannot be trusted, that God isn't good. That tactic dates back to

---

22 C.H Spurgeon, "Truth Stranger than Fiction," The Spurgeon Library, May 30, 1886; spurgeon.org/resource-library/sermons/truth-stranger-than-fiction/ (accessed April 15, 2025).

the Garden of Eden, when he convinced Eve that God was withholding something good. He wants you to believe that God is holding out on you and that the world has more to offer. His lies often mirror what we long to hear—they feel like enlightenment, empowerment, or the solution we've been waiting for. But Satan's goal is always the same: to pull us away from God. I promise you, even when doubt clouds your vision, God is for you and has good plans for you.

When doubt rears up, start with the resurrection. The empty tomb declares that *this is real*. Jesus didn't just rise from the dead; he did it for *you*. His victory over death proves that God is who he says he is, that his promises hold, and that your suffering is never the end of the story. If you're struggling to trust God, look to the cross and the resurrection. There you'll find the greatest proof of his love and the unshakable hope that he is working all things—even this—for your good. If he loves you enough to send his Son to die and rise for you, he is not going to let go of you in this, or ever.

I realize that right now, hearing that God loves you may sound hollow. Walking away from faith may sound tempting. But leaving now means enduring the pain without ever experiencing the joy God can bring through it.

The apostle John stood at the foot of the cross. He witnessed the worst—Jesus' suffering and death—yet he wrote more about God's love than any other disciple. He recorded Jesus' words, "As the Father has loved me, so have I loved you. Abide in my love" (John 15:9), and he was the one who declared, "God is love" (1 John 4:8).

If you press into God instead of walking away, you'll know his love from experience, not just academically. So please stay, even when it's hard and you feel abandoned. My friends who have continued to trust God through their

divorce have understood and experienced his love in a way that has marked them forever. Like the apostle John, they *know* God's love.

WAITING FOR SPRING TO COME

After my ex left, I had to place my hope in God himself, not in a specific outcome. For so long, I'd prayed that my marriage would not end in divorce. When it did, I wasn't sure what to do next—the future I had envisioned was gone. I didn't know what to hold on to anymore. I kept going back and forth, struggling to believe that things would change. I kept looking for signs that winter was almost over. I kept holding on, though sometimes by a thread.

One day when I felt particularly discouraged, my reading plan took me to Song of Solomon. I'll be honest, I expected to skim over the passage because the book's poetic mystery is generally beyond me. Here is what I read:

> *Arise, my love, my beautiful one, and come away, for behold, the winter is past; the rain is over and gone. The flowers appear on the earth; the time of singing has come. (Song of Solomon 2:10-12)*

Those words captivated me. I lingered over every phrase, sensing that God was inviting me to see myself as beloved and to trust that spring was coming, even though I'd seen no signs of it yet. Then I did something I'd never expected to do—I pinned verses from Song of Solomon on my bulletin board and prayed for their fulfillment. And over time, I started believing that change would come; I just needed to hold on.

If you are in the middle of winter, know that spring is coming. But change often unfolds slowly—a bloom here, a sunny day there—rather than arriving all at once.

There is a postscript to the story of that verse in my life. Six years after my ex left, I married Joel. I share more of our story in my memoir,[23] but one moment stands out above the rest. On our wedding day, we each independently wrote letters to one another. Amazingly, we both ended our letters with that same verse that I'd pinned to my bulletin board years earlier. That verse became a recurring theme in our celebration. My sister concluded her rehearsal dinner speech with it, and Joel's surprise wedding gift to me was a beautiful plaque engraved with those very words.

For me, that verse wasn't primarily pointing to Joel—it was a powerful reminder of God's faithfulness over the six years in which, bit by bit, winter had turned to spring. Meeting Joel was a beautiful part of my story. But our relationship wasn't what made my life whole. Spring doesn't come because of a merely human relationship; it comes because of God's faithfulness and his transforming work in our lives, whether we remarry or remain single.

THIS WILL BRING GOOD

Your divorce may feel as if it burned everything you cherished to the ground. But just as controlled fires enrich the soil, clear the way for new growth, and let in the sunlight, God can use the fires in your life to transform you. As Joni Eareckson Tada, a quadriplegic who was injured in a diving accident, said, "God permits what he hates to accomplish what he loves."[24] God grieves over the pain you've endured and are enduring, but through it, he is bringing beauty—for you, in you, and through you.

---

23 Vaneetha Rendall Risner, *Walking Through Fire: A Memoir of Loss and Redemption* (Nelson Books, 2020).

24 Joni Eareckson Tada and Steve Estes, *When God Weeps: Why Our Sufferings Matter to the Almighty* (Zondervan, 1997), p. 84.

I've seen this in my own life. Though I didn't understand it at the time, God was shaping me through the fire. I've grown more compassionate, knowing firsthand the ache of simplistic answers during suffering. My faith has deepened, and God's presence has become more real. Scripture came alive, and I met God through its pages. When everything I put my identity in was stripped away, I realized those things didn't and couldn't define who I truly was. My identity was in Christ, and he was all I needed.

As the Samaritan woman in John 4 turned the pain of five marriages that ended into a powerful testimony of the goodness and sufficiency of the Messiah, I've seen how sharing my own story of God's faithfulness has encouraged others to trust him as well. I've seen that my suffering wasn't wasted. Neither is yours. Having walked through heartache, you can especially comfort others, showing them what true care looks like. You know the loneliness and loss, but you also know the hope. You've experienced God carrying you when you were too weak to walk. That empathy is a gift that can build bridges where others see barriers.

Most of my friends who have walked through divorce say they wouldn't want to return to their former lives. They've learned they are strong, wise and resilient. They've experienced God's restoration and redemption. And they've felt God's love more intimately than before.

YOUR HONORABLE DISCHARGE

Moving forward takes time, and it certainly doesn't mean pretending that the past didn't happen. It means acknowledging what you've been through and recognizing that a season has ended. For some, that brings relief; for others, it feels like failure. Either way, closing this chapter with intention can help you step into what's next.

A friend once told me she wrote an "honorable discharge" from her marriage when her divorce was finalized—her way of marking the end of one season and the beginning of another. If that idea resonates, here's an example:

> *"You fought for your marriage. You gave your best. You stayed when it was hard, loved when it wasn't easy, and held on longer than most would have. You are forgiven for what you need to be forgiven for, and the rest is not yours to carry. And now, that chapter has closed. You are stepping forward in faith, trusting that God still has more for you."*

Just as a soldier's honorable discharge marks the completion of one calling and the beginning of another, so does this moment in your life. You are not walking away in defeat. You are walking forward in grace, knowing God is still at work.

The goal in writing your honorable discharge isn't to erase what was but to release yourself from carrying it forward in the same way. Because, no matter what has been lost, God is not finished.

THE PROMISE OF RESTORATION

Remember the exiles in Jeremiah's day? God had declared to them ahead of time that change would come: "Remember not the former things, nor consider the things of old. Behold, I am doing a new thing; now it springs forth, do you not perceive it? I will make a way in the wilderness and rivers in the desert" (Isaiah 43:18-19). No matter where you are today in your journey of healing, God has already begun to do something new. God is making a way through the wilderness.

The fire that burned through your life may feel as if it's left only ashes. But these ashes will not have the last word.

I echo the words of Elisabeth Elliot: “Of one thing I am perfectly sure: God’s story never ends with ashes.”[25]

I don’t know exactly what your story will hold, but I do know this: God is faithful. He will bring beauty from the ashes, joy from the mourning, and a hope that endures. As you wait, keep trusting and walking by faith, even on the hardest days when you can’t yet see the restoration ahead. His promises hold true for those who cling to him. You cannot know what the next chapter of your story holds, but you know the one who does. Your story ends in his presence, in a place beyond pain, where you’ll be whole, healed, and home. Trust him—spring is coming and, beyond it, everlasting joy.

25 Elisabeth Elliot, *These Strange Ashes* (Revell, 2004), p. 11.

QUESTIONS FOR PERSONAL REFLECTION OR DISCUSSION

This guide can be used for either personal reflection or discussion—you can go through it on your own, with a friend, or as part of a group. Don't feel you have to answer every question; focus on the ones that feel most helpful or relevant right now.

CHAPTER 1: THE UNDOING

1. What parts of this chapter could you most relate to, and why?
2. When have you felt most unseen or misunderstood in the aftermath of your divorce?
3. What moments have unexpectedly stirred grief—perhaps a place, a movie scene, or a casual comment? How did you respond in that moment?
4. What questions about faith or God have surfaced for you since your divorce?
5. In what ways have you found yourself "explaining" your divorce—to others or to yourself?

6. How is your relationship with the Lord? Is it closer, more distant, or the same as it was before the divorce? Where do you want it to be?
7. What would progress look like for you in this season? Using the check-in chart, which area feels most in need of attention—and what's one small step you can take?

CHAPTER 2: TEARS, FEARS, AND THE TENDERNESS OF GOD

1. Which emotions described in this chapter—shock, anger, shame, doubt, sadness, relief, grief, or fear—most resonate with you right now?
2. What messages have you internalized from others (or from yourself) since your divorce?
3. How have your emotions caught you by surprise—either with their intensity or timing? What did those moments reveal about your grief?
4. In what ways have you experienced ambiguous loss in your divorce?
5. What fears are you facing? List all that you can think of. What would it look like for you to replace those "what ifs" with "even if"?
6. Have you ever practiced lament? If so, how did that impact your faith? If not, what's held you back, and how do you think that might have impacted your faith?
7. If you're up to it, use the format in this chapter (p. 45) to write your own lament. Reflect on what you're feeling and bring it honestly before God.

CHAPTER 3: LETTING GO WITHOUT GIVING IN

1. What does "detaching" look like in your life right now?
2. When you think about forgiveness, what's your immediate reaction—resistance, guilt, longing, confusion? How does the chapter's definition of forgiveness affect the way you think about it?
3. Has bitterness taken root in your heart in any way? If so, what have the effects been?
4. Where are you on the journey of forgiveness?
5. Boundaries are important but can feel difficult to establish. What boundaries might help protect your peace or support your healing?
6. What has been your biggest challenge in navigating conflict with your ex-spouse? What strategies from the chapter could help you approach future conflicts more calmly and with greater wisdom?
7. What could healing look like for you? What would freedom from the past mean for your future?

CHAPTER 4: THE LIES WE BELIEVE AND THE GRACE THAT WE NEED

1. What untrue beliefs about your worth or identity have taken root after your divorce? What truths from Scripture speak directly to those lies?
2. Do you tend to blame yourself for too much or excuse yourself too quickly? How can you begin to sort through what's truly yours to own and what isn't?
3. What are some of the unhealthy ways you've tried to find relief or comfort?

4. How has your pain impacted your relationships—with your children, friends, or community? What might you need to repair?
5. What does repentance mean to you right now? Is there anything you feel nudged to surrender?
6. Have you found it hard to trust God since your divorce? What questions or doubts are you carrying? Take some time to talk to God about them.
7. As you reflect on the parable of the prodigal son, which son do you identify with most? What does it look like for you to "come home" to the Father—not in shame, but in trust and repentance?

CHAPTER 5: REASSESSING, REBUILDING, AND REKINDLING JOY

1. How does the image of hidden roots and unexpected regrowth in that chopped-down camellia encourage or challenge you right now?
2. Where are you in the rebuilding process—pausing, planning, grieving, resisting, or slowly laying bricks? What does it look like day to day?
3. Where have you sensed God inviting you to settle into your current place rather than longing for the past? In what areas are you still waiting to return to "what was" instead of asking God what might be next?
4. As you reflect on the six areas (Faith, Fun, Fitness, Finances, Family, and Friendships), what feels most draining? What areas sound easiest to start rebuilding in, even in small ways?
5. What parts of your situation would it be helpful to reframe—not to minimize the loss but to recognize God's work in it?

6. How would you describe your relationship with God right now? Dutiful? Distant? Growing? Honest? Have you been able to carve out time to linger with God instead of rushing past him?
7. What brings you joy—or used to? If you had a "fun brainstorm" session like the one described in this chapter, what would be on your list?

CHAPTER 6: PARENTING ON EMPTY

1. What have been your biggest fears for your children through this season? How have those fears shaped the way you parent or pray for them?
2. How has divorce impacted your children? What have been their greatest fears and struggles?
3. Where have you seen God give you wisdom or strength as a parent? Think about specific moments, large or small, where you sensed God helping you.
4. What role has prayer played in your parenting? What Scripture(s) could you pray specifically for your children's needs?
5. What parenting expectations—of yourself or your children—do you need to release? Do you feel pressure to "prove" that you're doing okay or that your children are fine?
6. How can you nurture your children through this season? What intentional steps can you take this week to encourage connection, express love, or offer grace?
7. What have been the most difficult parts of coparenting for you? Are there any changes you want to make after reading this chapter?

CHAPTER 7: THE CHURCH, THE CROWD, AND THE FRIENDS WHO STAYED

1. When do you feel most lonely these days? How has that changed since the divorce—and what has helped (or might help) to ease that loneliness?
2. Have you experienced the difference between loneliness and solitude? What helps you move from feeling alone to feeling grounded in God's presence?
3. In what ways has misplaced shame tried to define you? What truths from this chapter—or from Scripture—can help you reframe your identity in Christ?
4. How has the church supported or hurt you during this season? If you've been wounded, what might help you reconnect—or seek healing?
5. What has community looked like for you in this new season of life? Have certain relationships faded or deepened? What kind of support do you need most right now?
6. What voices are shaping you most right now—friends, social media, podcasts, books? Are they drawing you closer to God or pulling you away? If you sense a drift, what practical changes could help you re-center your focus?
7. Where are you still longing to belong? What's one brave step you could take toward finding connection, whether in your church, friendships, or neighborhood?

CHAPTER 8: DATING AND THE R WORD

1. Do you feel pressure—internally or externally—to get remarried? What do you think is motivating that pressure? How is it impacting you?
2. If you're considering dating, what values or boundaries do you want to hold on to? What would it look like to honor God and yourself in a future relationship?
3. Would you be willing to invite a trusted friend to help hold you accountable in your dating relationships—or even help you write a profile, if you're considering online dating? If so, jot down a few possible names and what you'd ask them to do.
4. Some believe you should only date if you're ready to remarry; others see dating as part of figuring that out. Where do you land? If you're unsure about remarriage, how might you communicate that clearly—and why does that matter?
5. What's your personal mission statement for this next chapter of life? If you haven't written one, what core values or priorities would you want it to include?
6. How do you feel about the idea of staying single—either for now or for good? Is there fear, peace, or something in between?
7. What does it look like to trust God with your future relationships—or your singleness? What would help you live with hope while staying rooted in contentment?

CHAPTER 9: HOPE ON THE HORIZON

1. Where have you seen evidence of God working through the "fires" in your life? What have you learned, even through pain, that you may not have seen otherwise?
2. What verses, promises, or pictures of hope are helping you hold on? Is there a "Song of Solomon" moment you've clung to—or one you're still waiting to see?
3. Is walking away from faith tempting for you? What is fueling that, and how can you resist that temptation? What truths do you need to remind yourself of in those moments?
4. What's one area of your life where you long to see God restore what was lost? Are there any small signs of that restoration already—or anything you hope to see in time?
5. If you were to write an honorable discharge for yourself, what would it say?
6. How might God use your healing to encourage someone else? What have you walked through that could become a gift to others? Is there anyone you can encourage right now?
7. Can you trust that God is still writing a good story with your life—even after divorce? How could believing that shift the way you see your past, your present, and what's still ahead?

APPENDIX 1

HOW TO SHOW UP WHEN A FRIEND'S MARRIAGE ENDS

Let me start by saying thank you—thank you for being willing to read this and for wanting to care for a friend walking through the aftermath of divorce. It means so much when someone steps in—even briefly—during a season when many step away.

As you read, remember you're not expected to do everything. You can't. And if you feel responsible for fixing your friend's problems, you may end up overwhelmed—and unintentionally make things harder for them. Trust that God knows what they need and will supply it. Pray about what to do, and step into whatever God is calling you to do—however big or small—with faith.

You may feel uncertain or unqualified, unsure if you have the time or skills to help. That's okay. As Ed Welch says, "If you feel quite weak and ordinary—if you feel like a mess but have the Spirit—you have the right credentials. You

are one of the ordinary people God uses to help others."[26]

Walking alongside someone may require sacrifice, but it can also be a tremendous blessing. More often than not, I've walked away just as encouraged as the person I was there to support, because the Holy Spirit met us both. As Proverbs 11:25 reminds us, "Those who refresh others will themselves be refreshed" (CEB).

If you're not sure how to start deeper conversations, consider reading this book with your friend and working through the questions on pages 147-155. The questions are designed to help your friend process what's happened and open the door to more meaningful support (you can feel free to pick and choose the ones which seem most helpful). Whether you're a close friend stepping in regularly or a more casual friend offering occasional help, both roles matter. I hope you'll keep checking in.

This appendix is divided into two parts. The first is for friends walking alongside someone they know personally. In Appendix 2, you'll find a form to give your friend to fill out, to help you better understand their needs. (There's also a companion form for you to clarify what you're able and willing to offer.) If this format feels more transactional than personal, you may prefer to use these questions as a jumping point to talk things through or write in a note. But however you do it, you'll find that clear expectations help everyone feel better supported and understood.

The second section is directed to churches and outlines practical ways for members and leaders to provide compassionate care. There's a separate questionnaire in Appendix 2 to help church leaders know what support is most needed.

---

26 Edward Welch, *Side by Side: Walking with Others in Wisdom and Love* (Crossway, 2015), p. 13.

Whoever you are—friend, ministry leader, or someone who simply cares—I encourage you to read both sections. Together, they offer a fuller picture of how to care well.

PART 1: FOR FRIENDS

One of the greatest gifts you can offer a friend going through divorce is your presence—through your words, your actions, and your willingness to stay. The acronym SHOW UP can help you remember how to care in ways that matter:

- *S — Show Up.* Be present and consistent, whether in person or from afar.
- *H — How Is Today?* Ask specific, thoughtful questions that invite honesty.
- *O — Offer Specific Help.* Don't just offer in general—name what you're able to do.
- *W — Words of Encouragement.* Speak truth that builds up without minimizing their pain.
- *U — Use Active Listening.* Pay attention in a way that helps them feel truly seen.
- *P — Pray. Ask God for wisdom.* Keep lifting your friend up to him as you walk together.

SHOW UP

This is the most meaningful thing you can do. It doesn't always mean showing up physically—though that's a gift—but it does mean making the effort to stay present in your friend's life: sending a quick check-in text, picking up

the phone, sitting with them in silence, or remembering them on days that might feel extra heavy.

Showing up isn't a one-time thing. It matters that you keep showing up. Support often pours in early, but friends naturally return to their routines—often just when loneliness and exhaustion peak. Divorce recovery isn't quick or linear, but your ongoing presence can bring deep healing.

If consistency isn't possible, that's okay—just be honest about what you can offer. Divorce can heighten fears of abandonment, so following through matters. If you need to cancel plans or can't respond, initiate another time. One friend said, "Every coffee date you forget or text you don't reply to stings a little more when someone already feels forgotten. Don't underestimate the healing power of consistency."

My sister always picked up the phone when I called. If she was busy, we wouldn't talk too long, but it felt so comforting to know that I could count on someone. One divorced friend would call one of her closest friends on the way to work every day and just check in for a few minutes. Touchpoints like that remind people that they are not alone.

WHAT SHOWING UP CAN LOOK LIKE

In person (if you're local)

- Stop by to talk or invite them for coffee or a meal.
- Go to church together and plan something low-key afterward.
- Accompany them to hard events—court, reunions, or a child's music recital.
- Take a walk—side by side often feels easier than face to face.

- Set a regular rhythm: a weekly walk, a monthly dinner, a consistent text thread.

From a distance (if in-person is not feasible)

- Send a text or call them—especially on weekends or at night.
- Set up a regular phone or video check-in.
- Read this book with them and talk through a chapter each week (or however frequently they'd like) using the questions starting on page 147.
- Offer to be a "point person" to help organize support from friends, so that the weight isn't all on them.

HOW IS TODAY?

One of the best ways to support your friend is to keep checking in—but not with the usual "How are you?" That question can feel too broad to answer, especially in the middle of heartache. Most people will answer, "I'm fine" when they are barely hanging on, either because they don't know how to put their pain into words or because they're not sure anyone really wants to hear about it.

That's why asking something more focused, like "How is today?" can be more helpful. It invites honesty without demanding a full update. Your friend may still talk about the week or what's ahead, but starting with today keeps the question manageable. Ask because you care, not because you need a detailed answer. And don't stop asking—your interest, not their response, is what matters most.

Here are five specific questions that can help your friend feel seen:

1. How has today been for you?
2. What's something that surprised you recently—good or hard?
3. What do you need most right now—someone to listen, practical help, or a break from it all?
4. Is there a part of your story you wish someone would ask about or take time to understand?
5. What's on your plate this week that feels heavy? Is there anything that you're dreading or hoping for?

OFFER SPECIFIC HELP

In the wake of divorce, the emotional toll is heavy, but so is the logistical load. Meals still need to be made. Children still need rides. The laundry doesn't stop. And often, your friend has no idea of what to ask for—or how.

That's why offering specific, tangible help is one of the kindest gifts you can give. It doesn't have to be big—just specific. Well-meaning offers such as "Let me know if you need anything" are generous in intent, but they place the burden back onto the person who's already overwhelmed. A clear offer, especially when you give a couple of options, removes that pressure and often sparks ideas for what they might need, especially when they don't even know what to ask for yet. Even one thoughtful offer can go a long way.

For ongoing needs, one idea that can help everyone involved is to set up a group text that includes your friend and a few others willing to help (often 4-8 people works best). Your friend can share needs—like a ride, a meal, or just needing company—and a separate thread with the helpers can coordinate who's available. That thread can

also be used to remember important dates or remind one another to check in.

To avoid silence, someone in the group can respond quickly in the main thread with "Thanks for sharing—everyone's checking their schedules, and we'll follow up soon." If no one is able to help, a message like "We couldn't coordinate help this time, but we're so glad you reached out—we're still here for you," helps close the loop with care.

Here's what offering help might sound like:

- "Can I bring dinner on Tuesday? Or is there a better day—and do you have any preferences?"
- "I love doing laundry. Would it help if I picked yours up on Friday and dropped it back folded?"
- "I've got two hours on Monday. Would it help if I ran errands for you, watched your kids, or went with you to run errands?"

WAYS TO HELP

Everyday Needs

- Bring a meal or send a gift card.
- Pick up groceries or help with errands.
- Tackle a small project together like organizing paperwork.
- Handle home tasks: repairs, yard work, tech issues, or car maintenance.

Parenting Support

- Watch the kids occasionally or regularly.
- Be a backup for school pickups, projects, or homework.

- Invite their children to hang out with your family.

Relief for What's Overwhelming

- Be their "phone-call person" in hard moments.
- Help with emails, paperwork, or résumés.
- Offer budgeting help or assistance navigating insurance.
- Send gift cards for essentials—or for a small treat.
- Invite them into your holidays.
- Ask if they need a break, and help make it happen.
- Help with care appointments—find providers, offer childcare, or contribute financially.

WORDS OF ENCOURAGEMENT: WHAT TO SAY (AND NOT SAY)

After a divorce, many people feel invisible—so words of encouragement matter more than ever. Encouragement isn't about solving their problems or offering advice. It's about reminding them that they're seen and valued, and not forgotten by God.

We often feel pressure to cheer people up, but true comfort doesn't sound like clichés or forced optimism. Proverbs 25:20 says, "Whoever sings songs to a heavy heart is like one who takes off a garment on a cold day, and like vinegar on soda." Both images are jarring. Taking off your coat leaves you exposed, and vinegar on soda causes a small explosion—disruptive and messy. When someone is grieving, false cheer can feel the same way. Often, the most loving thing we can do is acknowledge what's hard and stay with them in it.

Mutual encouragement strengthens both people. Don't

treat your friend like a project. If they invite you in, share your life too. Trust their wisdom and don't assume their spiritual life is on pause.

Encouragement can come in many forms—meeting in person for a meal or a visit, sending a text or voice memo, mailing a card or writing a short note. One of the most meaningful things someone did for me was gathering encouraging notes from friends and compiling them in a small scrapbook. I'm pretty sure I wore out the binding on that as I paged through it on hard days.

We often wonder what to say—and what to avoid. Here are some suggestions:

WHAT TO SAY

- "This is devastatingly hard. It's heartbreaking for me too, and I'm standing with you."
- "You're doing a great job. I see how you're showing up and doing the hard work." (Though be sensitive to whether your friend wants affirmation for being courageous and strong or the freedom to acknowledge they are anxious or angry.)
- "I noticed you did ____________." (Share something specific that you want to commend).

WHAT NOT TO SAY

- "At least..." (Any sentence that starts this way will likely feel minimizing or dismissive.)
- "Our friend went through this too—and her situation was worse." (Comparison is not helpful.)
- "You should..." or "Have you tried...?" (Unsolicited advice often feels like veiled criticism.)

Don't assume their divorce is a spiritual problem. You can encourage them to trust the Lord, but be sensitive as you do it. For more on this, see the church section.

USE ACTIVE LISTENING

One of the best ways to support someone is simply to show up and listen. Your friend needs a safe space to be honest, without judgment or quick answers. Listening means making space for grief—asking thoughtful questions, receiving their story with care, and resisting the urge to rush toward the bright side.

Job's friends started well, sitting with him in silence for seven days because they saw how great his suffering was (Job 2:13). But when they spoke, they began to analyze and correct. Job responded, "Listen closely to what I'm saying. That's one consolation you can give me" (Job 21:2-3, NLT) and, "Do you intend to rebuke my words, when the words of one in despair belong to the wind?" (6:26, NASB). In suffering, words aren't always tidy. Let your friend speak freely. Some words are meant to be carried away by the wind.

HOW TO LISTEN WELL

- Give your full attention: Put away your phone. Don't multitask. Make eye contact.
- Let silence linger. Your friend may need time to find the right words. Don't rush them along.
- Affirm what they're saying with words like "That sounds overwhelming" or "It makes sense that you feel that way."
- Reflect what you hear by repeating or summarizing it. This can help your friend process their own thoughts.

- Ask follow-up questions. This isn't to jump in with solutions but to go deeper on their train of thought.
- Listen again next week and the week after that. Grief takes repetition—and that's okay.

CAUTIONS WHILE LISTENING

- Don't interrupt with your own stories or comparisons.
- Don't minimize their pain by trying to move them forward too fast.
- Some people process internally and may not want to talk while others may offer a cascade of words. Honor both.
- Don't ask for details they haven't offered.

PRAY

Prayer isn't what we do when we've run out of options—it's the most important and powerful thing we can offer. It brings the needs of our friend to the only one who can truly help. Before anything else, begin here.

Start by praying for yourself. Ask God for wisdom, strength, compassion, and the faith to trust that he's working, even when you can't see it. Pray that you won't shrink back from what God is calling you to or take on what he hasn't called you to. It's easy to say we'll pray and never do it, so build it into your day. Perhaps set a timer for three minutes and pray specifically for your friend. You might be surprised by how much you can cover in just three focused minutes.

You can pray that your friend would be protected from shame, fear, bitterness, and isolation; that their children would experience comfort and stability; that practical needs

would be met; and that God's presence would feel near. Praying Scripture is especially powerful. Try inserting your friend's name into a verse, which could look like this: "Lord, would you supply every need of Jordan's according to your riches in glory in Christ Jesus" (Philippians 4:19). Other helpful passages to pray include Isaiah 41:10, Joshua 1:9, Psalm 34:18, Romans 15:13, and Psalm 23:1–3.

Ask your friend specifically, "How can I pray for you?" and pray right then if they're open to it. You might even set up a time to pray weekly, either alone or with a few trusted friends.

WAYS TO ENCOURAGE THROUGH PRAYER

- Text a verse you're praying so they can join you in it.
- Name the specific needs you're lifting up.
- Take a picture of a Bible passage you're praying over them and text it.
- Pray a psalm of lament together—like Psalm 13 or 142. As outlined in chapter 2, read a few verses, and then follow the psalmist's model, starting with complaint, moving to requests, and ending in trust.

PART 2: FOR THE CHURCH

BE WELCOMING

The church should be one of the safest, most supportive places for people walking through any kind of pain, including divorce. But that's not always the case. Too often individuals and families feel forgotten, judged, unsure of whether and how they belong. As the body of Christ, we're called to pursue the hurting, help carry their burdens, and care for people in crisis.

Here are four ways church members can show up for people through and after divorce. In each, there are suggestions for church members first and then for pastors or lay leaders.

1. MAKE YOUR CHURCH A PLACE OF WELCOME AND COMPASSION

As with individuals, the most meaningful support the church can offer is often to simply be there for divorced people. We aren't their Savior. We can't solve all their problems, deepen their faith, or change them. But we can walk beside them, offer what we are called to, and trust God with the rest.

If you see someone sitting alone in church, sit with them or invite them to sit with you. Initiate a conversation. Invite them to lunch after service if you can or follow up with them later. And if they reach out for coffee or a phone call, please say yes. They probably already feel vulnerable asking, and rejection likely feels all the harder now. Encourage hospitality teams to notice those sitting alone and take the initiative to reach out.

Most divorced people feel vulnerable walking into church. They are often carrying more than grief—there's shame, fear, regret, anger, and deep questions about identity and belonging. Divorce can make people feel judged or pushed to the margins of the church, but you can counter that by showing up, listening without assumptions, and inviting them into real community. You don't need to know the whole backstory to invite someone to Bible study or out for coffee—your kindness can make all the difference in their view of the church. Anna Meade Harris writes:

> *"We often don't welcome divorced families with open arms, but rather with a whole lot of questions. While there is a moral dimension to divorce, we must not take it on ourselves to figure out what happened to the marriage and why."*[27]

She suggests leading with invitation rather than investigation, which often closes the door before people have had the chance to step in. Instead of asking, "What happened in your marriage?" try "How has divorce affected you?"

If you're a church leader and know members who've walked through divorce, ask if they'd be willing to connect with someone who is early in the process. You could keep a quiet list of "divorce mentors"—trusted men and women who aren't professional counselors, but who have experienced God's faithfulness and are open to meeting one-on-one. When someone new shares that they're going through divorce, you might simply say, "Would it help to talk with someone who's been there?" That kind of connection can make a world of difference.

Be willing to sit with survivors of abuse and offer support as they begin to process what's happened to them or their children. Abuse is a painful and complex issue, but it's one the church must be willing to step into with both compassion and care. As counseling pastor and author Brad Hambrick, says, "Most counseling mistakes arise from the questions we don't ask."[28] In these situations, asking thoughtful questions and offering steady presence matters deeply. I echo Rachael Denhollander's words:

---

27 Anna Meade Harris, *God's Grace for Every Family: Biblical Encouragement for Single Parent Families and The Churches That Seek to Love Them Well* (Zondervan, 2024), p. 24.

28 Ed. Brad Hambrick, *Becoming a Church That Cares Well for the Abused* (B&H, 2019), p. 21.

> *"My prayer for you is that the depth and beauty of the gospel is made increasingly more real, and that you begin to both feel the enormous weight of ministering to the wounded, and also the incredible hope you can be equipped to bring."*[29]

2. POINT PEOPLE TO THE LORD WITHOUT BEING PRESCRIPTIVE

Divorce often creates a spiritual crisis. Some feel abandoned by God; others wonder if they still belong in church. It's a season when faith may deepen or unravel. It is the church's role to offer compassion and comfort as members walk through grief and questions. As Jude 22 reminds us, we are to "have mercy on those who doubt."

Much of suffering remains a mystery this side of heaven, and Scripture invites us to weep with those who weep, rather than trying to explain away their grief. Divorce is especially tender territory, and well-intended attempts to make sense of someone's pain often feel dismissive. Even Scripture, when used like a hammer, can hurt rather than heal. Instead of offering verses as answers, share how they met you in your own pain, briefly and with humility. Saying, "This verse ministered to me when I was struggling—it may not help you, but I wonder if it might" is very different from "Here's what you need to believe."

If it feels appropriate, consider inviting someone walking through divorce to a prayer time, Bible study, or reading plan. Let them ask questions and express doubts without rushing to answer them. Lament (introduced in chapter 2) may be especially meaningful—praying a psalm of lament together can give voice to grief while anchoring hope.

---

29 As above, p. 14.

Don't assume that someone going through divorce has less to offer spiritually. Pastors and leaders may want to look for ways to include divorced members in meaningful service—not only after they've "healed" but as they walk with God in real time. This may be a time of growth and deep dependence on God. Consider gently affirming how their experience might encourage others.

3. HELP SHEPHERD THE CHILDREN

Some of the most damaging fallout from divorce is felt by children, who often blame themselves but rarely receive direct care. The church has a powerful opportunity to support these young people, not by singling them out but by consistently showing up in their lives. That simple act reminds them that the church isn't just for intact families—it's for them too.

Single parents often feel that the full weight of their children's futures and faith rests on their shoulders. As one friend told me:

> *"My divorce is one thing. But the effect of divorce on my kids? That's what keeps me up at night."*

One of the best ways to support single parents is to pay attention to their children. One mom said:

> *"Every time someone greets my child by name, it reminds me we're not invisible. It reminds me I'm not raising them completely alone."*

One way to help carry the load for single parents is to offer to pray regularly and specifically for one child.

Children grieve differently than adults. Their pain may look like acting out, withdrawing, or pretending they're fine. Be compassionate and supportive, considering their needs rather than seeing them as burdens or problems.

One family regularly invited my daughters to dinner and made them feel seen. Years later they still talk about it. It wasn't flashy, but it made them feel like they belonged.

Here are some practical ways to care: learn their names, make a point of saying hello, and ask about their lives. Invite them into your home for dinner.[30] Offer rides to school or practice, or help coordinate a small team to rotate. Cheer them on at games, concerts, or recitals. Help with homework, school projects, or college applications when you can. Small acts of presence can speak louder than any program. Even something as small as taking them for ice cream once a month can mean the world. For teens especially, a steady mentor can make a lasting difference. If you can't be that person, try to connect them with someone who can.

If you're in youth ministry, keep an eye out for students navigating divorce at home. Their families may look different from others in the group, and they may feel out of place. Take time to meet with them individually and connect them with peers or mentors who will stay present. They need to know they matter and that others will stay, even when things feel hard. Showing up for them now could shape how they see God for years to come.

4. HAVE A PLAN TO HELP WITH NEEDS

While the church often responds quickly to crises like illness or loss, it can fall silent when a family breaks apart. Divorce is often complex—the fallout stretching over months or years—and it rarely comes with a clear end date. Legal battles, court dates, childcare struggles,

---

30 In any way that you seek to support children who are in this position, make sure you know and are following legal guidelines and the safeguarding policies your church has in place, and that you are being wise in the way you interact with children and youth who are in a vulnerable place emotionally.

financial stress, and emotional fallout can accumulate quickly. Often, people in the church simply don't know how to help.

That's why intentional care from the church matters so much. One of the most practical ways to offer support is by forming a care team to help carry the load. My pastor did that for me, dividing tasks among friends who could offer rides, fix computer issues, make repairs, or commit to pray. (See the "O" section for friends on pages 162-163.)

Ideally, someone in leadership—whether a pastor, elder, deacon, men's or women's ministry leader, or discipleship director—should take the lead in caring for divorced members. Needs will vary: some may be looking for work, others might benefit from intentional mentoring, and many will face one-time or ongoing financial challenges. Since most people won't feel comfortable asking for help, it's a tremendous gift when the church initiates those conversations.

Practical obstacles like lack of childcare or transportation, or cost often prevent single parents from participating in church events. Ask what would make it easier for single parents to attend and consider how your church can help remove those barriers. More broadly, many divorced individuals feel they no longer fit in. Churches can shift that by creating low-pressure, relational environments—like shared meals or informal gatherings—where people of all backgrounds can connect without feeling out of place.

Support doesn't have to look the same in every church. As Anna Meade Harris writes:

> *"A very small congregation in rural Iowa probably will not have the personnel or finances (or need) to construct an entire program of support for single parents, but it might*

be able to keep a notebook in the church office where members can catalog the kinds of help they can offer. Or a well-organized lay leader can connect helpers with families, which also helps members grow in relationship and affection ... the challenge for the larger congregation is developing true friendship between members so that help does not become more transactional than relational."[31]

Some elements of a care plan could include...

- offering benevolence funds for upcoming bills, counseling, legal help, children's school needs, or childcare.
- keeping a list of trusted Christian counselors, lawyers, and mediators.
- pairing single parents with small groups or families for ongoing support.
- connecting newly divorced individuals with others who have walked through divorce—whether for regular mentoring or just a one-time conversation.
- distributing the "How the Church Can Help" form to better understand and meet people's needs.
- designating a point person (in leadership or lay ministry) to follow up and regularly check on updated needs and to coordinate help.
- offering peer-support groups. If the church isn't equipped to lead one, be familiar with trustworthy groups like DivorceCare (see if that's hosted in your area) and refer people there proactively. Consider hosting it if there's interest.

31 Anna Meade Harris, *God's Grace for Every Family*, p. 128.

The most important thing is not having a perfect plan—it's having a plan at all. Being proactive says, "You're not alone. You're still part of us. We care."

I know how hard it is to know what to say or do when someone you care about is walking through divorce. That's why I wrote this appendix—not to give a formula but to offer a few practical ways in which you can come alongside someone in a vulnerable time. Small things make a big difference. I pray that through you, they'll glimpse the kindness and faithfulness of Jesus.

APPENDIX 2

SOME HELPFUL FORMS FOR COMMUNICATING WITH FRIENDS AND CHURCH

You can find ready-to-use downloadable versions of these at thegoodbook.com/communicationhelp or by scanning this QR code:

FORM 1: FOR SOMEONE WALKING THROUGH DIVORCE TO GIVE TO FRIENDS ON WHAT WOULD BE MOST HELPFUL

Hi friend,

Thank you for being someone I can trust. I know it can be hard to know how to help, so I put together a few things that would be especially meaningful or helpful right now. I'm not expecting you to do everything—just sharing this in case it gives you a clearer idea of where I could use support. I'm so grateful you're walking with me in this.

Name: ______________________

Preferred way to contact and contact info:

____

☐ Text ☐ Call ☐ Email

Best time of day: ________________

HOW OFTEN I'D LIKE TO HEAR FROM SOMEONE

☐ A few times a week ☐ Weekly ☐ Monthly

WHAT MIGHT HELP

EMOTIONAL SUPPORT

☐ Check in with me

☐ Listen and help me process decisions

☐ Send encouraging verses or notes

PRACTICAL HELP

☐ Meals

☐ Groceries or errands

- [ ] Laundry, cleaning, yard work, computer help.
  Describe ______________________________
- [ ] Childcare
- [ ] Budgeting or paperwork
- [ ] Résumé or job help
- [ ] Gift cards for food, gas, or groceries
- [ ] Ride to court, church, school (for kids) or appointments
- [ ] Other _______________________

SPIRITUAL ENCOURAGEMENT

- [ ] Read the Bible or a devotional with me
- [ ] Invite me to church or Bible study
- [ ] Help me navigate spiritual questions
- [ ] Pray regularly for me and with me
- [ ] Ground me in godly truths and help me battle doubt

SUPPORT FOR MY KIDS

- [ ] Spend time with them
- [ ] Help with schoolwork
- [ ] Attend their games or activities
- [ ] Pray for them

SOCIAL SUPPORT

- [ ] Invite me for coffee or dinner

- [ ] Include me in weekend or holiday plans with your family
- [ ] Save me a seat at church
- [ ] Include me in singles or 1-1 activities

WHAT'S NOT HELPFUL RIGHT NOW:

____

IF I HAD TO NAME JUST 2-3 THINGS THAT WOULD BE MOST HELPFUL RIGHT NOW, I'D CHOOSE...

1.
2.
3.

THERE WASN'T A PLACE IN WHICH TO MENTION THIS EARLIER, BUT I'D LIKE YOU TO KNOW...

FORM 2: FOR FRIENDS ON WHAT THEY ARE ABLE TO OFFER

Hi friend,
I care about you and want to walk with you in this season—but I also know I can't do everything. To make things a little easier on both of us, these are specific things I'm able to offer right now. My hope is that this helps you know what you can count on, and that it brings even a little relief along the way.

Name: ______________________________

Preferred way to contact and contact info:

____

☐ Text ☐ Call ☐ Email

Best to reach me: ____________________

HOW OFTEN I'M ABLE TO CHECK IN OR HELP

☐ A few times a week ☐ Weekly ☐ Monthly

☐ As needed

HOW I CAN HELP

TIME-BASED HELP

☐ Drive to appointments or church

☐ Babysit or give rides to children

☐ Help with errands

☐ Drop off meals (fresh or frozen)

☐ Regular check-ins (text or call)

☐ Have you over for a meal or coffee at my house

SKILL-BASED HELP

- ☐ Laundry or housework
- ☐ Yard work or small repairs
- ☐ Job search or résumé help
- ☐ Financial or budgeting advice
- ☐ Tech or computer help
- ☐ Pastoral/counseling support

SUPPORT FOR CHILDREN

- ☐ Regularly spend time with one child/mentor
- ☐ Occasionally spend time with one or more children
- ☐ Help with schoolwork
- ☐ Attend games or events
- ☐ Take children for outings or weekends
- ☐ Buy clothes or other necessities for school or sports

SPIRITUAL SUPPORT

- ☐ Pray with you and share encouragement
- ☐ Read Scripture or a devotional together
- ☐ Pray. Send me a list of prayer requests weekly
- ☐ Be a sounding board to listen and process faith questions

OTHER

- ☐ Contribute financially to needs (or help pool resources with others)
- ☐ Be a point person to organize others (meals, rides, care teams)
- ☐ I'm open to being asked about other needs

HOW I PREFER TO HELP

- ☐ I prefer to give behind-the-scenes help (errands, research, organizing)
- ☐ I'm available for in-person support
- ☐ I do better with flexible tasks I can do on my own time
- ☐ I prefer to respond as needs arise
- ☐ I'm fine with a regular rhythm (weekly/monthly check-ins, coffee dates, etc.)

THESE ARE THE 2-3 AREAS OF SUPPORT THAT FEEL MOST DOABLE OR NATURAL FOR ME TO OFFER RIGHT NOW:

1.
2.
3.

BOUNDARIES AND CONSTRAINTS I NEED TO BE HONEST ABOUT:

FORM 3: FROM SOMEONE WALKING THROUGH DIVORCE ON HOW THEIR CHURCH CAN HELP

This form is simply a tool to help you share where you could use care and support. While the church may not be able to meet every need—and we know we'll often fall short—we want to be intentional in how we walk with you. Your responses help us understand what matters most to you, so we can better come alongside you as part of the body of Christ. Please fill it out as you're able, knowing you are seen, valued, and not alone.

Name: ______________________________

Preferred way to contact and contact info:

____

☐ Text ☐ Call ☐ Email

Best time of day: _____________________

1. HOW OFTEN I'D LIKE TO HEAR FROM SOMEONE:

☐ Daily ☐ A few times a week

☐ Weekly ☐ Monthly/Occasionally

NAMES AND AGES OF CHILDREN (IF APPLICABLE):

2. WHAT TYPE OF CARE WOULD BE MOST HELPFUL RIGHT NOW? CHECK ALL THAT APPLY

EMOTIONAL/RELATIONAL SUPPORT

- ☐ Regular check-ins.

  Circle preferences: text... call... or in person.
  Frequency: weekly... monthly... quarterly

- ☐ Encouragement
- ☐ Help finding a counselor
- ☐ Someone to listen

PRACTICAL SUPPORT

- ☐ Meals (fresh or freezer)
- ☐ Childcare or help with school transportation
- ☐ Errands (groceries, pharmacy, etc.)
- ☐ Housework or laundry
- ☐ Yard work or home repairs
- ☐ Financial support or help managing a budget
- ☐ Résumé help or job-search support
- ☐ Gift cards (groceries, gas, takeout)

SUPPORT FOR MY KIDS

- ☐ Rides to/from activities
- ☐ Mentoring or regular time with a trusted adult
- ☐ Invitations to family dinners or outings

- [ ] Help preparing for milestones (college, jobs, birthdays, etc.)
- [ ] Help nurturing their faith

SOCIAL SUPPORT

- [ ] Invitations for holidays or church events
- [ ] Someone for our family to sit with at church
- [ ] Regular meals or coffee with someone
- [ ] Help finding community at church

3. WHAT IS NOT HELPFUL OR WELCOME RIGHT NOW?

This helps us avoid doing things that add stress instead of relieving it.

4. ARE THERE ANY SPECIFIC NEEDS OR CIRCUMSTANCES YOU'D LIKE US TO KNOW ABOUT?

5. HOW CAN WE BEST SUPPORT YOU SPIRITUALLY RIGHT NOW?

☐ Pray for me—by text, call, or in person.

Optional: something specific I'd like prayer for is

____

☐ Invite me to study Scripture or read something together

☐ Invite me to church or Bible study

☐ Help me navigate my doubts or questions about faith

☐ Other ______________________ ______________________

6. IF YOU COULD ONLY PICK 2-3 THINGS THAT WOULD BE MOST HELPFUL RIGHT NOW, WHAT WOULD THEY BE?

1.

2.

3.

7. ANYTHING ELSE YOU'D LIKE TO SHARE?

ALTERNATE FOR FORM 1

If you're the one asking for a "what's helpful" form from your divorced friend, here's a way to preface it.

Dear friend,
I know it can be hard to ask for help—or even to know what kind of help would be helpful right now. This simple form is just a way to name what you're carrying and what kind of support might ease the weight. You don't have to check every box—just the things that feel most needed or doable in this season. This is helpful for friends who want to help but aren't sure what you need. You're not a burden. You're loved. And your honesty will help others walk with you more intentionally.

ALTERNATE FOR FORM 2

If you're the divorced person asking a friend to fill out the availability form, here's a way to preface it.

Dear friend,
Thank you for your willingness to show up. This short form is a way to clarify what you're able to offer—so that expectations are clear and no one feels overwhelmed. You don't need to do everything to make a real difference. I'm not expecting you to. In fact, naming your availability honestly is one of the most loving things you can do. I'd love to talk about it with you when you've had a chance to fill it out.

APPENDIX 3

HELPFUL BIBLICAL RESOURCES

ARTICLES[32]

1. Jim Newheiser, "What Does the Bible Teach About Divorce and Remarriage?" The Gospel Coalition, July 15, 2024; thegospelcoalition.org/article/bible-divorce-remarriage/

2. Wayne Grudem, "Grounds for Divorce: Why I Now Believe There Are More Than Two" in *Eikon* (CBMW), Spring 2020; waynegrudem.com/grounds-for-divorce-why-i-now-believe-there-are-more-than-two

3. Greg Gifford, "A Response to Wayne Grudem's Paper on a Third Reason for Divorce," Biblical Counseling Coalition, January 13, 2020; biblicalcounselingcoalition.org/2020/01/13/a-response-to-wayne-grudems-paper-on-a-third-reason-for-divorce/

32 All articles accessed July 10, 2025.

4. John Piper, "Divorce and Remarriage: A Position Paper," Desiring God, July 21, 1986; desiringgod.org/articles/divorce-and-remarriage-a-position-paper

BOOKS

1. H. Wayne House, ed., *Divorce and Remarriage: Four Christian Views* (IVP US, 1990)
2. Mark L. Strauss, ed., *Remarriage After Divorce in Today's Church: 3 Views* (Zondervan, 2006)
3. David Instone-Brewer, *Divorce and Remarriage in the Church: Biblical Solutions for Pastoral Realities* (IVP, 2006)
4. Jim Newheiser, *Marriage, Divorce, and Remarriage: Critical Questions and Answers* (P&R Publishing, 2017)
5. Wayne Grudem, *What the Bible Says About Divorce and Remarriage* (Crossway, 2021)

ACKNOWLEDGMENTS

Carl, this book wouldn't exist without you. You prayed about it before I did and had to insist I pray too. Why that felt like a novel idea for me, I'm not sure. I'm grateful I got to work with such a wonderful editor, as well as the whole team at The Good Book Company.

Austin, you continue to be the best agent I could have asked for—patient, responsive, and always supportive.

Aly and Jenny, you keep me on track and somehow never get tired of my Instagram questions. I don't know what I'd do without you both.

Lindy, Alison, Karen, Kathryn, Christa, Monica, Lauren, Howard, Margot, Melissa, Kristian, Jim, and Jess—friends who have also walked through divorce—thank you for sharing your stories with me. I learned so much from each of you, and your words are woven throughout this book (without names, of course, to protect our shared secrets).

Melanie, my dear friend and college roommate, I'm especially grateful for the hard-won insight that made this book better. Thank you for reading every chapter, laughing at my snarkiness, and catching things I didn't even know needed catching.

D, my ex-husband, I'm grateful we're friends. Forgiveness has changed all of us, and made family gatherings a lot less awkward.

So many friends and family members walked with me through my divorce that I won't mention everyone by name, partly because I'd never live it down if I forgot someone. I hope you know who you are because your fingerprints and pep talks are all over these pages. You leaned in when many would have stepped back, and I'll always be grateful. Jennifer, I mentioned you in the book, and I could have filled an appendix with the ways you and so many others showed up for me.

Mom and Dad, I know my divorce was painful for you too. You carried your own grief with mine, and I'm so grateful for your love and support. Thank you for walking with me, praying for me, and for all the ways you encouraged me (even when my stubborn streak probably made it harder).

Shalini, my sister and closest friend, I don't know how I would have survived without you. You've helped me with much of my public writing, been the best closet redecorator I could have asked for—complete with mediocre Panera coffee, great conversation, and cardboard boxes you graciously didn't leave in the rain—and always answered the phone even when you saw my number. You could have single-handedly written the first appendix, because you lived it.

Katie, you stood beside me when everything was falling apart. You watched out for me, shouldered more than you should've had to, drove me everywhere once you turned 15, and offered endless grace (even when I kept giving you driving "advice" and insisted on printing out every song lyric before you could listen to it). Your strength, courage, and steadiness shaped more of this story than you know.

Kristi, you forgave me after I threw ice water on you and even celebrated me with a "MOMMY" acrostic—Y for "yelling less and less." You challenged me not to settle for pat answers, showed wisdom beyond your years, asked the best hard questions, and brought insight and humor to every chapter of this book. And you still make me laugh like no one else can.

Joel, every day I wake up amazed that God brought us together and that I get to be married to you. You encourage my loud off-key singing, put up with my (almost imperceptible) idiosyncrasies, and bring me beverages on demand. Thank you for making everything I do possible and for sacrificing for me in a million little ways. Through you, God has truly restored the years the locusts have eaten.

Much as I love and cherish these dear friends and family, my greatest joy—and the one I am most indebted to—is Jesus. Your love and grace are breathtaking. While my divorce was never my plan, I see how you used it for my good and your glory. Through it, you drew me closer than I ever could have imagined, and I am so thankful I'll never live one day without you. To you be the glory.

BIBLICAL | RELEVANT | ACCESSIBLE

At The Good Book Company we are dedicated to helping Christians and local churches grow. We believe that God's growth process always starts with hearing clearly what he has said to us through his timeless and flawless word—the Bible.

Ever since we opened our doors in 1991, we have been striving to produce resources that are biblical, relevant, and accessible. By God's grace, we have grown to become an international publisher, encouraging ordinary Christians of every age and stage and every background and denomination to live for Christ day by day and equipping churches to grow in their knowledge of God, their love for one another, and the effectiveness of their outreach.

Call one of our friendly team for a discussion of your needs or visit one of our local websites for more information on the resources and services we provide.

Your friends at The Good Book Company

I0606107